THE LORD'S SUPPER

52 READINGS WITH PRAYERS

K. M. HADDAD

K. M. Haddad

OTHER BOOKS BY THIS AUTHOR

CHRISTIAN LIFE
Applied Christianity: Handbook 500 Good Works
You Can Be a Hero Alone
Worship Changes Since 1st Century + Worship 1sr Century Way
The Best of Alexander Campbell's Millennial Harbinger
Inside the Hearts of Bible Women-Reader+Audio+Leader
The Lord's Supper: 52 Readings with Prayers

BIBLE TEXTS
Revelation: A Love Letter From God
The Holy Spirit: 592 Verses Examined
Was Jesus God? (Why Evil)
365 Life-Changing Scriptures Day by Date
Love Letters of Jesus & His Bride, Ecclesia (Song of Solomon)
Christianity or Islam? The Contrast
The Road to Heaven

FUN BOOKS
Bible Puzzles, Bible Song Book, Bible Numbers

TOUCHING GOD SERIES
365 Golden Bible Thoughts: God's Heart to Yours
365 Pearls of Wisdom: God's Soul to Yours
365 Silver-Winged Prayers: Your Spirit to God's

SURVEY SERIES: EASY BIBLE WORKBOOKS
→Old Testament & New Testament Surveys
→Questions You Have Asked-Part I & II

HISTORICAL RESEARCH BIBLE
for Novel, Screenwriter, Documentary & Thesis Writers

HISTORICAL NOVELS & STORYBOOKS
Series of 8: They Met Jesus
Ongoing Series of 8: Intrepid Men of God
Mysteries of the Empire with Klaudius & Hektor
Christmas: They Rocked the Cradle that Rocked the World
Series of 8: A Child's Life of Christ
Series of 10: A Child's Bible Heroes
Series of 8: A Child's Bible Kids
Series of 10: A Child's Bible Ladies

GENEALOGY: Climb Your Family Tree w/o Falling Out
Volume I & 2: Beginner-Intermediate & Colonial-Medieval

Cover by **Bryan Minear** on **Unsplash**
Copyright © 2019 K. M. Haddad

NORTHERN LIGHTS PUBLISHING HOUSE, ISBN- 978-1-952261-13-8
All rights reserved, including the right to reproduce this book or portions thereof in any form without author's permission.
Bible quotations are taken from the International English Bible
Printed in the United States

The Lord's Supper: 52 Readings with Prayers

INTERNATIONAL ENGLISH BIBLE TRANSLATION COMMITTEE

INTERNATIONAL BIBLE TRANSLATORS, INC is comprised of a small core of Bible scholars who specialize in Biblical Hebrew, Aramaic, and Greek, and in lexicography and linguistics.

The chairman of the translation committee of The INTERNATIONAL ENGLISH™ BIBLE is Dr. Stanley L. Morris. He served as an editor in the Translations Department of the **American Bible Society** from 1968 to 1972 under the world-famous linguist, Dr. Eugene A. Nida, a true pioneer in the field of Bible translation. While in New York City, Dr. Morris was also privileged to work directly with the renowned New Testament scholar, Dr. Bruce M. Metzger of **Princeton University**.

Over the 37 years that the **International English™ Bible** was in the making, more than 2,000 people have reviewed this new translation — from Hebrew, Greek and other Bible Scholars to average Bible students. All of their advice has been taken into consideration to publish a Bible that the whole family can easily understand and enjoy.

The **International English™ Bible** is translated directly and accurately from the best original Greek, Aramaic and Hebrew texts and manuscripts. Here is a A Partial List Of Scholarly Advisers To The *International English™ Bible*.

Stanley L. Morris, Ph.D (chairman)
F. W. Gingrich, Ph. D (famous Greek lexicographer)
Jack P. Lewis, Ph. D in Old Testament from Hebrew Union and Ph.D. in New Testament from Harvard
Hugo McCord, Th.D.
Clyde M. Woods, Ph.D.
S. K. Kang, Ph.D. (world-class expert in Sumerian)
Gary T. Burke, Ph.D.
Milo Hadwin, D.Min.
Larry Quinaltry, Ed.D.
Benjamin Goldstein, Orthodox Rabbi

K. M. Haddad

HOW THIS BOOK WAS WRITTEN

Most obvious, this book was written in large type so it can be more easily read publicly.

The scripture readings were organized alphabetically by Bible Book name except for week one which begins in Genesis and the first sin and ties it in with the cross. Week two begins with readings from Acts and Week fifty-two ends with readings from Zechariah.

Readings do not have to be done in the order they appear in this book.

It is illegal to quote the Bible for 95% of a published book unless that version was never copyrighted (i.e., KJV). I did not want to paraphrase the scriptures. Therefore, I obtained permission from the legal owner of the International English Bible, Sheila Morris, the widow of Dr. Stanley E. Morris, chairman of the IEB translation committee. The IEB is also recorded on a single MP3 which is perfect for listening in your vehicle. Here is their website in case you would like to order a copy of the Bible yourself. http://bit.ly/2LZNd03

The Lord's Supper: 52 Readings with Prayers

TABLE OF CONTENTS

Other Books by this Author 2
International English Bible Translation Committee 3

How this Book Was Written.. 4
Why 52?.. 7
Week 1.. 16
Week 2.. 19
Week 3.. 21
Week 4.. 23
Week 5.. 26
Week 6.. 29
Week 7.. 31
Week 8.. 34
Week 9.. 36
Week 10.. 39
Week 11.. 42
Week 12.. 45
Week 13.. 48
Week 14.. 51
Week 15.. 54
Week 16.. 57
Week 17.. 60
Week 18.. 64
Week 19.. 67
Week 20.. 70
Week 21.. 73
Week 22.. 76
Week 23.. 79
Week 24.. 82
Week 25.. 84
Week 26.. 87
Week 27.. 90
Week 28.. 93

Week 29.. 95
Week 30.. 98
Week 31.. 101
Week 32.. 104
Week 33.. 107
Week 34.. 110
Week 35.. 113
Week 36.. 116
Week 37.. 118
Week 38.. 121
Week 39.. 123
Week 40.. 126
Week 41.. 128
Week 42.. 132
Week 43.. 134
Week 44.. 136
Week 45.. 138
Week 46.. 139
Week 47.. 142
Week 48.. 144
Week 49.. 145
Week 50.. 149
Week 51.. 152
Week 52.. 155

Thank You... 158
About the Compiler 159

Buy Your Next Book Now 160
Connect With The Author 161

Get A Free Book.. 161
Join My Dream Team 161

The Lord's Supper: 52 Readings with Prayers

WHY 52?

We get our authority and example of how often to keep the Lord's Supper in Acts 20:7. Let's take a close look at it:

⁷On Sunday, we all met together
to eat the supper of the Lord.

Notice the word THE. Is that significant? Let's look at another similar passage in the Old Testament. It's one of the Ten Commandments:

⁸Remember the sabbath day, to keep it holy.

How did the Jews interpret THE? Did they keep the sabbath day holy once a month, quarterly, yearly? We know they interpreted THE as meaning each and every without exception.

EVEN IN THE GREEK

Still not convinced? Let's look at original language Luke wrote Acts of the Apostles in.

Some translations of the Bible say "On the first day of the week" they met to "break bread." Let's break verse 7 down.

WHEN

The only passage that talks directly about when the early Christians kept the communion is Acts 20:7 that says the church met on the first day of the week TO (for the purpose) BREAK BREAD.

Below is the sentence in Greek working down, with English meanings next to each Greek word.

'*En* = During
***de* = and**
***ta* = observe, keep commandment or regulation**

According to the concordance, the word "*ta*" is another word for "*ho*." Both words mean affairs of something or the state of something. According to *Vine's Expository of N.T. Words*, "*ta*" means an official regulation or commandment regarding the affairs or state of something.

***mia* = every first**

According to the concordance, "*mia*" is the feminine form of "*heis*". "*Heis*" is translated "one" 283 times.

"*Mia*" is translated "first day." This word refers to "each" or "one by one" or "every one."

So this word refers not only to it being the first day, but one particular day which was regarded during each week.

"*ton*" = certain day, particular day
This word does not appear alone in Greek sentences. It is part of a hyphenated term "*mia-ton*."

In the front of the concordance under "first," "*mia*" was translated "first (day)." Above that under "First, at (the)". It was translated from the Greek term "*pro-ton*." It gives the significance of copying another first, an original first, a prototype.

There are only three significant events for Christians involving the first day of the week in the New Testament; Jesus rose from the dead on the first day of the week, Jesus returned to heaven on the first day of the week, and the church began on the first day of the week. Therefore, to the Christian, this would be a particular day kept every week in memorial.

Sabbaton = **first day after the Sabbath**

FOR WHAT?

sunag-menon = **religious assembly (from same root word as synagogue)**

harmon = **espoused or adopted**

"***Hermo-zomai***" in the back of the concordance refers to doing something in harmony with something else. Vine's *Expository of New Testament Words* says the word "***harmon***" refers to something that is PERPETUAL and ongoing as in EACH AND EVERY such day perpetually.

WHO?

So, who partook of the Lord's Supper? Early in chapter 20, Luke (the author of Acts) said there were Paul and him present. Then in verse 4 he says Sopater, Aristarchus, Secundus, Gaius, Timothy, Tychicus and Trophimus met Paul and Luke in Troas (near the famous Troy of Greek mythology).

They stayed in Troas seven days. On Sunday "we all met together to eat the supper of the Lord. Who were "we all"? Verse 7 says Paul preached to midnight. Verse 8 says they were in an upstairs room and verse 9 says they were on the third floor. Verse 8 says there were many torches indicating that everyone attending had a torch so they could find their way home in the dark, so there were many people who belonged to the many torches.

Who served the Lord's supper to them all? Did Paul? Did Timothy? It does not say. Therefore, how they got the elements of the Lord's Supper into their mouth did not matter.

However, there are groups who declare only priests can put the bread into the mouth of worshippers. So, who are Christian priests? They are all Christians.

I Peter 2:5 says,
*⁵You also are like living stones. God is using you to build a spiritual house, so that you will be a holy **group of priests**, offering spiritual sacrifices which God will gladly accept through Jesus Christ.*

I Peter 2:9 says,
*⁹Nevertheless, you are a chosen race, **a royal group of priests**, a holy nation, and a special people. You must tell about the wonderful things that God has done. He called you from darkness into His amazing light.*

Revelation 1:4-6 says
*"⁴From John. To the seven groups in the land of Asia (Roman province in today's western Turkey) who have answered God's call.... Jesus loves us. He bled, setting us free from our sins. He formed us into a kingdom. **We are priests to God, his Father.**"*

WHY?

They met TO break bread. Was it a meal or a ceremony?

Acts 2:46 says the Christians broke bread daily from house to house gladly. Tracing the verse in Greek....

"metalam" = *metabolism.* meaning to receive food to nourish the body.
"prophe" = meat and means nourishment.

So, they ate food for their nourishment from house to house.

But in Acts 20, the bread they ate was unleavened ceremonial bread. They ate *"artoned"* bread.

arton = **bread, translated shewbread in the Jewish religion.**

The "shewbread" in the Old Testament was made without yeast.

Leviticus 24 and I Chronicles 23 explain how to make the "shewbread".

¹Yahweh said to Moses....⁵"Take flour and bake twelve loaves of bread with it. Use four quarts of flour for each loaf. ⁶Put them in two rows on the pure gold table [in the tabernacle/temple] in My presence. Six loaves will be in each row.... ⁸Every sabbath day, in My presence, Aaron will set the bread in order. This covenant with the people of Israel will always continue....

²⁹They were responsible for putting out the holy bread on the table, for the flour in the grain-offerings, and for the bread made without yeast. They did the baking and the mixing, too. And, they did all the measuring.

But the practice originated with the first and actual Passover when God passed over the houses in Egypt that had the blood of the lamb on their doorposts. Let's look at Exodus 12 and the importance of the bread having no yeast.

¹*Then Yahweh spoke to Moses and Aaron in the land of Egypt:*
²*"This month will be the most important month for you. It will be the 1st month of the year for you....*

¹¹*Also, this is the way you must eat it: Have your robe tucked in your belt, have your shoes on your feet, and have your staffs in your hands. You must eat the meal in a hurry. It is My Passover.* ¹²*I will pass through the land of Egypt on that night. I will strike down all the firstborn ones in the land of Egypt—human and animal. I will carry out judgments against all the gods of Egypt. I am Yahweh!* ¹³*The blood on the houses where you are will be a sign for you. When I see the blood, I will pass over you. There will be no disaster among you to destroy you when I strike down the land of Egypt.* ¹⁴*This day will be one for you to remember. You must celebrate it as a festival to Me. You must celebrate it throughout your generations. This is a permanent command.' "*

....¹⁴*This day will be one for you to remember. You must celebrate it as a festival to Me. You must celebrate it throughout your generations. This is a permanent command.' "*

¹⁵*"For seven days you must eat bread which has no yeast in it. By the first day, you must have surely gotten rid of any yeast in your homes. If anyone eats anything which contains yeast during those seven days, then that person will be cut off from Israel...*

¹⁷*"You must celebrate the Feast of Unleavened Bread, because I brought your divisions out of the land of Egypt on this very day. Therefore, you must celebrate this day throughout your generations as a permanent command.* ¹⁸*On the 1st month, on the 14th day of the month, in the evening, you must eat bread which contains no yeast until the evening of the 21st day of the month.* ¹⁹*No yeast will be found in your houses for seven days. If anyone eats anything with yeast in it, then that person must be cut off from the congregation of Israel—whether he is a foreigner or native-born.* ²⁰*You must eat nothing with yeast in*

it. In all your homes, you must not eat anything which contains yeast.'"

The Passover was also called The Feast of Unleavened Bread. The day before Passover began, every bit of yeast was swept out of the house.

When Jesus instituted the Lord's Supper, he was keeping the Passover. Luke 22:1 explains, *¹It was almost time for the Feast of Unleavened Bread, called the Passover Festival…. ⁷The day came for the Passover Feast. This was the day when the priests sacrificed the Passover lambs. ⁸Jesus sent Peter and John, saying, "Go and prepare the Passover meal for us to eat."*

FIGURATIVE YEAST

Also, leaven was referred to by Jesus as representing sin and error. Matthew 16 is one passage explaining this:

⁵When Jesus' followers went across Lake Galilee, they forgot to bring along some bread. ⁶Jesus said to them, "Be careful! Watch out for the yeast of the Pharisees and the Sadducees."

….¹¹Why could you not understand what I said to you!? When I said, 'Watch out for the yeast of the Pharisees and the Sadducees,' I was not talking about literal bread." ¹²Then they understood that Jesus was not wanting them to stay away from the yeast used for literal bread. Instead, he wanted them to avoid the teaching of the Pharisees and the Sadducees.

Paul referred to the yeast of sin in I Corinthians 5.

⁷Clean out the old yeast of sin, so that you may become a new batch of dough. Then you will be pure. Christ, our Passover lamb, was sacrificed. ⁸So, let us celebrate our Passover Festival, but not by using the old yeast – that is, the yeast of sin and of evil. Instead, let us use the non-yeast of sincerity and truth.

Therefore, the significance of leaven continued in the Christian era, and unleavened bread for the Lord's Supper was always used.

NOT A MEAL

Verse 11 says after midnight, they broke bread again. But this time it was for a meal.

After he broke off some of the bread and ate it, Paul spoke to them a long time. When he finished speaking, it was early morning.

He (and perhaps the others also) broke bread and ate.

geuomai = ate, tasted

This was not a religious ceremony (**sunag-menon**), but a regular meal.

WHAT ELSE?

Besides remembering the body and blood of Jesus during our communion with him, we are to examine ourselves. Let's look at Paul explanation in I Corinthians 11:

[23]I received from the Lord what I passed on to you: During the night that the Lord Jesus was betrayed, he took bread. [24]Then he thanked God for it and broke off some of it. Jesus said, "This bread is[d] my body which I am giving for you. Eat this to remember me." [25]After supper, Jesus took a cup in the same way. He said, "This cup is the new covenant with God in my blood. Drink this to remember me. Every time you drink this, you will be remembering me." [26]Every time you eat this bread and drink from this cup, you are telling about the Lord

Jesus' death, until he returns.

²⁷So, if anyone eats the bread or drinks the cup of the Lord with the wrong attitude, then he will be guilty of sinning against the body and the blood of the Lord Jesus Christ! ²⁸Each person must look deeply into his own heart. Then he should eat of the bread and drink from the cup in the right way. ²⁹If someone is eating and drinking without recognizing the meaning of the body of Christ, then he is condemning himself by eating and drinking! ³⁰This is why many of you are weak and sick. A large number of you have died, too. ³¹If we judged ourselves, then we would not be judged. ³²No, it is the Lord who judges us. We are being corrected, so that we will not be condemned with the people of the world.

Did we crucify Jesus anew in the past week? Are we willing to look deep inside our hearts at our motives and what is most important to us? Are we planning to do better?

This weekly self-examination prepares us for the Big Final Exam at the Judgment Seat of God.

CONCLUSION

Christians are to meet together on the first day of every week perpetually for the primary purpose of breaking ceremonial bread (communion) in honor of the first time (in harmony with ~ **hermo-zomai**) the original (**pro-ton**) as a prototype of when Jesus instituted the ceremony.

Scriptures show they worshipped in other ways too. They prayed, preached, read scriptures, sang. In fact, they could and did do these things throughout the week.

But Acts 20:7 indicates the primary purpose for meeting on Sunday was to keep the communion to "remember the Lord's death until he comes" (1Corinthians 11:26).

WEEK 1

HIS BODY

[14]Then the Always-Present One, God, said to the snake, "Because you have done this thing…I will put hostility between you and the woman, between your children and her child. You will bite his heel but her child will crush your head.…

[35]The angel said to Mary, "The Holy Spirit will come upon you and the power of the Highest One will cover you. The holy baby will be called 'God's Son.'"

[14]The "children" are human. So, Jesus himself also shared in their humanity. He wanted to use death to destroy the Devil who has the power of death. [15]Jesus also wanted to set all people free from the slavery of fearing death all their lives.

[31]The time has come for this world to be judged. The time has come for the ruler of this world to be thrown out.…[8]Since the beginning, the Devil has been sinning. The person who continues to sin belongs to the Devil. Why did the Son of God appear? To destroy the Devil's works.

PRAYER

Lord God, so long ago when Adam and Eve sinned, you set in motion a Plan to get us away from Satan's control.

You created us and wanted us back. For thousands of years you promised to save us from Satan forever. We didn't understand why it took so long, but finally the time came. Jesus stepped foot on earth so he could save our souls. We thank you for keeping your promises. We thank you for Jesus' willingness to die on that terrible cross for us.

HIS BLOOD

[9]The large dragon was thrown out. (This is the old snake who is the same as the one called the Devil, Satan. He is the one who fools the whole world.) He was thrown down to the earth. He and his angels were thrown out. [10]I heard a loud voice in heaven say: "Now the salvation, the power, the kingdom of our God, and the authority of His Christ have come, because the accuser of our brothers has been thrown out. [11]But they have defeated him because of the Lamb's blood.

. 18Christ suffered and died for your sins once for all time. He was a righteous man dying for bad men.... But when Jesus suffered and died, he was "crowned with glory and honor." By God's gracious love, he did this to taste death for every person.

Victory has swallowed up death. [55]Where is your victory, O Death? Where is your power to hurt, O death?" [56]Sin is death's power to hurt. Sin gets its strength from its relationship with the law of God. [57]But, thank God, through our Lord Jesus Christ, God gives us the victory!

K. M. Haddad

PRAYER

How can we thank you enough, oh God, for keeping your promise to ransom us from Satan with the blood of Jesus? What a terrible price, but you were determined. Your love for us, though sinners we are, was victorious. And now, because of the blood of Jesus, we are yours. Thank you.

Genesis 3:14; John 12:31; Luke 1:35; I John 3:8; Hebrews 2:14; Luke 22:19-20; Revelation 12:9-11a; I Peter 3:17; Hebrews 2:9; I Corinthians 15:55-57

WEEK 2

HIS BODY

Jesus from Nazareth was a very special man. God clearly showed this to you. God proved this by the powerful and amazing things which He did through Jesus among you. You yourselves know this is true. [23]You killed this man Jesus by handing him over to lawless men. They nailed him to a cross. But God knew ahead of time that all this would occur; it was part of His plan which He made long ago. [24]Jesus suffered the pains of death, but God set him free. God raised Jesus up from death. It was impossible for death to hold him....

PRAYER

Lord, we think back to that day two thousand years ago when fickle men loved Jesus one day and demanded his crucifixion two days later. In many ways, that describes us. We claim we love you, then when it comes time to prove it, we put you second in our lives. We think back to the day he offered his body as a sacrifice to ransom us from Satan. We will spend the rest of our lives thanking you.

HIS BLOOD

[32]So, Jesus, not David, is the one whom God raised from death! We are all eye-witnesses of this! [33]Jesus was lifted up to heaven. Now Jesus is with God—at His

right side. The Father has now given the promise of the Holy Spirit to Jesus. So now, Jesus poured out this which you see and hear. ³⁴David did not go up to heaven. It was Jesus. David himself said:

> 'The Lord God said to my Lord.
> "Sit at My right side
> ³⁵until I put your enemies under your feet." '

³⁶Therefore, all the people of Israel can be sure of this one thing: God has made Jesus both Lord and Messiah, this man whom you nailed to the cross!"

PRAYER

Father, in some ways we, too, crucified Jesus that day so long ago. The sins of mankind ~ both before and after ~ were taken on Jesus who took the blame for them all. Then Jesus took the punishment for them. His blood was the only thing that could ransom us from Satan. How terrible was the price, but Jesus paid it. How you love us. How we love you. Thank you.

Acts 2:22b-24, 32-36

WEEK 3

HIS BODY

²³I received from the Lord what I passed on to you: During the night that the Lord Jesus was betrayed, he took bread. ²⁴Then he thanked God for it and broke off some of it. Jesus said, "This bread is my body which I am giving for you. Eat this to remember me." ²⁵After supper, Jesus took a cup in the same way. He said, "This cup is the new covenant with God in my blood. Drink this to remember me. Every time you drink this, you will be remembering me." ²⁶Every time you eat this bread and drink from this cup, you are telling about the Lord Jesus' death, until he returns.

PRAYER

Our Lord, we can only imagine what you went through that night, telling your closest friends to eat what represented your body and blood. We wonder if your apostles refused at first because they didn't want you to die and begged you with tears not to let it happen. When we today eat this bread, sometimes we, too, weep. You gave so much to ransom us from Satan.

HIS BLOOD

²⁷So, if anyone eats the bread or drinks the cup of the Lord with the wrong attitude, then he will be guilty of sinning against the body and the blood of the Lord

Jesus Christ! [28]Each person must look deeply into his own heart. Then he should eat of the bread and drink from the cup in the right way. [29]If someone is eating and drinking without recognizing the meaning of the body of Christ, then he is condemning himself by eating and drinking! [30]This is why many of you are weak and sick. A large number of you have died, too. [31]If we judged ourselves, then we would not be judged. [32]No, it is the Lord who judges us. We are being corrected, so that we will not be condemned with the people of the world.

PRAYER

Oh, God, when we look back on the previous week to see how we did, we have to face our sins. Satan is too strong for us. Satan convinces us that bad is so much fun, it is not really sin. We listen to his lies even though we do not want to. Give us strength and wisdom this coming week to do better and to remember your rules are only to keep us safe.

I Corinthians 11:23-32

WEEK 4

HIS BODY

[12]You were buried with Christ by immersion. You were also raised with Christ through believing in the power of God who raised Christ from death. [13]When you were spiritually dead in your sins.... God brought you back to life with Christ. He forgave all of our sins. [14]God wiped away the written code with its strict orders. It was negative; it was against us. He took it out of the way. He nailed it to the cross. [15]After God stripped away the power of the rulers and the authorities, He showed this openly, using the cross to show His victory over them.

[21]Christ never sinned, but God caused him to become sin for us, so that we could be right with God in Christ....[7]We have something in Christ—his blood has set us free. We have the forgiveness of sins! God's gracious love is so rich!

[4]God was rich in mercy, because of His great love which He had for us. [5]While we were spiritually dead in rebellion, God made us alive with Christ. (You have been saved by God's gracious love.)

PRAYER

Lord, thank you for giving us the gift of baptism, something physical we can do for a greater spiritual outcome, just like your crucifixion was something physical you did for a greater spiritual outcome. How were you able to stay sinless? How were you able to take onto yourself the blame and punishment for all our killing and cheating and torturing and every evil thing as though you had done them yourself? We do not understand such love. All we can do is say thank you.

HIS BLOOD

[13]You used to be far away, but now, in Christ Jesus, you have come near. This was made possible by the blood of Christ.... [12]For our fight is not against human beings. No, it is against rulers, against authorities, against world powers of this darkness, and against evil spiritual beings in the heavenly world.

[3]May God our Father and the Lord Jesus Christ be kind to you and give you peace. [4]Jesus sacrificed himself for our sins, so that we might escape from the evil in this present age. This is what God our Father wanted. [5]To God be the glory forever and ever. Amen.

[20]I was killed on the cross with Christ. So, the life which I now live is not really me—it is Christ living in me! I still live in my body, but I live by faith in the Son of God. He is the one who loved me; he sacrificed himself for me.

PRAYER

Our loving God, help us become so busy in your kingdom that we have less and less time to think about doing wrong. Help us search for ways to honor you in the world, to sacrifice for you in this world, to kill our egos in this world so that only Jesus lives in us.

Colossians 2:12-15; 2 Corinthians 5:21; Ephesians 1:7; Ephesians 2:4-5, 13; Ephesians 6:12; Galatians 1:3-5; Galatians 2:20

WEEK 5

HIS BODY

⁴⁶"People will sin against You—everyone sins.…²⁰Surely there is not a good person on earth, one who always does good and never sins.…

³But all have turned away. Together, everyone has become rotten. None of them does anything good —not even one person!

³But everyone had turned away. Together, everybody had become filthy. None of them were doing anything good —not a single person!

O Yahweh, hear my prayer! Listen to my cry for mercy! Come help me because You are loyal and righteous. ²Don't put me, Your servant, on trial because no one alive is innocent in Your presence.

PRAYER

Our heavenly Father, we are so embarrassed. We sing praises to you on Sunday, then go out and commit the same old sins on Monday. Over and over we commit the same sins, then blithely ask you to forgive us. How can you keep forgiving and forgiving and forgiving? All we can do is thank you for being merciful to us sinners who only try sometimes to do better.

HIS BLOOD

²³All have sinned and fallen short of the glory of God.

⁶While we were still helpless and ungodly, Christ died for us—at exactly the right time. ⁷It is rare when anyone dies for another person—even for a righteous person. However, there are instances when somebody dares to die for a good person. ⁸But God reassures us of His love for us in this way: While we were still sinners, Christ died for us!

⁹Since Christ's blood has now made us right with God, we will be saved even more so from God's punishment through Christ. ¹⁰We were God's enemies, but the death of His Son was used to make us God's friends. Now that we have become friends of God, we will be saved even more so by Christ's life. ¹¹Not only that, we feel good about being in God through our Lord Jesus Christ. We now have friendship with God through Christ.

PRAYER

Oh, Lord, right in the middle of all our rebellion against you, you died for us. We were your enemies, but you died for us. We do not understand such love. All we can do is thank you for it and ask that you help us get busy doing so many things for you, we do not have time for all the sinning.

I Kings 8:46a; Ecclesiastes 7:20; Psalm 14:3; Psalm

K. M. Haddad

53:3; Psalm 143:1-2; Romans 3:23; Romans 5:6-11

WEEK 6

HIS BODY

⁶Then Yahweh passed by in front of Moses and proclaimed: "Yahweh! Yahweh! I am a merciful, loving God who does not get angry easily. I abound in love and truth. ⁷I am loyal to thousands. Although I will forgive evil, rebellion, and sin, I will certainly not let the guilty ones go unpunished. I will cause the children and grandchildren to suffer for the sins of their ancestors to the third and fourth generation."

⁹So, know that the Always-Present One, your God, is the one true God! He is the faithful God. For 1,000 lifetimes, He will keep the covenant and be loyal to those people who love Him, to those who obey His commands.

²⁶"O God, You are loyal to those who are loyal. You are upright to those who have integrity.

PRAYER

Oh, Lord, we know you treat people the way we treat you. If we don't have time for you, you do not have time for us. If we don't want to talk to you in prayer, you do not want to answer. If we are loyal to you, you are loyal to us. But you go beyond that for people who have become Christians and are truly trying to do better. You love us despite our sins. You even died for us. Thank you. Thank you.

HIS BLOOD

[22]The Always-Present One's love never ends. His mercies never stop. [23]They are fresh every morning.
O God, Your faithfulness is great. [24]I say to myself, "The Always-Present One is what I've got. Therefore, I have hope, because of Him."

[18]There is no God like You. You forgive sin. You overlook the transgressions of God's people who are left. The Always-Present One will not stay angry forever. No, He takes delight in showing mercy.
[19]Yahweh will once again have mercy on us. He will conquer our sins. And, You, O God, will throw away all of their sins into the depths of the ocean.

PRAYER

Forgiveness, Lord, is not easy for you. You have to continually be snatching us away from Satan. So every day you forgive and forgive because you want us to live with you in your home. Oh, God, thank you for overcoming Satan while on the cross and when you returned to life. You are an amazing Savior and we thank you over and over.

Exodus 34:6-7; Deuteronomy 7:9; 2 Samuel 22:26; Lamentations 3:22-23; Micah 7:18-19

WEEK 7

HIS BODY

¹Long ago, God used the prophets to speak to our ancestors many times and in many ways. ²But, during these last times, God used His Son to speak to us. God appointed him to inherit everything. Through him, God also made the universe. ³The Son is the shining brightness of God's glory and the exact picture of God's real being. The Son holds up the universe by his powerful word. After he had provided a cleansing from sin, he sat down at God's right side in heaven.

⁴Jesus has received a title—Son. This is better than any of the angels. He is so much more important than angels. ⁵God never said this to an angel: "You are My Son. I have fathered you today." and again, "I will be his Father and he will be My Son."

¹⁰God also said this about His Son: "Lord, in the beginning, you laid the foundation of the earth. The heavens are the result of your work.

PRAYER

Our God, we are so lucky to be living after the time you materialized as the Son and came to earth instead of before when the prophets could only foretell your coming. We are lucky, also, to be living in a time when each one of us can have a copy of your very Words.

Thank you for explaining to us why you had to die. No one could do it for you ~ not the angels, not the prophets. It was your blood Satan wanted as our ransom. Thank you. Thank you.

HIS BLOOD

[11]But Christ has come as High Priest over good things which already exist. He went through the greater and more perfect Sanctuary It is not man-made. (This means that it is not a part of this world.) [12]Once for all time, Christ went into the most holy place and secured for others everlasting forgiveness from sin. He used his own blood, not the blood of goats or calves. [13]The blood of goats, bulls, or the ashes from a young cow are sprinkled upon unholy people. This makes them separate and clean on the outside. [14]But, how much more will the blood of Christ make our consciences clean from dead human efforts, so that we can worship the living God! Through the everlasting Spirit, Christ offered himself to God as a perfect sacrifice.

[24]Christ did not enter the most holy place which was man-made, a copy of the real one. No, he went into heaven itself to appear before God for us. He's there now....

But now, at the end of the ages, Christ has appeared to get rid of sin once for all time by sacrificing himself. [27]It is certain that all persons die one time. And, the Judgment Day comes after death.

PRAYER

Lord Jesus, you laid down on the altar of the world and died in our place. You created us, watched us destroy our souls, then cringed when Satan enslaved us. You brought us back to you, washed our souls in your blood, and made our souls white as snow. Thank you, Lord, Jesus. Thank you.

Hebrews 1:1-6, 10; Hebrews 9:11-14, 24, 26-28

WEEK 8

HIS BODY

7During Jesus' human life, he offered prayers to God. with strong cries and tears, Jesus asked God to save him from death. (God could have done it, too, but He didn't.) God listened to Jesus because Jesus was devoted to God. 8Even though Jesus was God's Son, Jesus learned to obey from the things he suffered. 9After Jesus was made perfect, he became the Source of eternal salvation for everyone who will obey him

[24]Jesus lives forever. He never passes on his priestly work to others. [25]So, Christ can completely save the people who come to God through him.

PRAYER

Our Lord, how hard it must have been for you to take the blame for every ghastly thing we ever did ~ some we bragged about and others we hid out of embarrassment and shame. You gathered the souls of the world to you on that day and told us you would take our punishment for us ~ all of us. We worship you and always will.

HIS BLOOD

Christ always lives to plead for us….. [28]In the same way,

Christ was sacrificed once for all time to take away the sins of many people.

[1]We are surrounded by such a large number of witnesses! We must put aside anything that might slow us down. Sin can easily tie us up. Let us run with endurance the race that is ahead of us. [2]Jesus endured when he had to suffer shame and die on a cross. Why? Because of the happiness that lay ahead for him. He didn't mind the way he had to die.

PRAYER

Oh, God, we are in a race against Satan. He tries to slow us down by throwing hurdles of temptation in front of us. He knows what are weaknesses are and wears us down. Sometimes we become so weak and want to just give up and stop. Don't let us, Lord. Run besides us until we reach Home.

Hebrews 5:7-9; 24-25, 28; Hebrews 10:1-2

K. M. Haddad

WEEK 9

HIS BODY

[1]Who would have believed what we heard!? Who foresaw Yahweh's power in this? [2]He grew up like a small plant in the presence of God. He was like a root coming up out of dry ground. He had no special beauty or splendor to cause us to notice him. There was nothing in his appearance to attract us to him. [3]He was hated and rejected by people. He endured much pain and suffering. People would not even look at him. He was hated, and we didn't think that he was an important man.

[4]But he certainly took our suffering upon himself, and he felt our pain for us. Though we saw his plight, we thought that God was punishing him. [5]But he was wounded for the things that we did wrong. He was crushed for the sinful things we did. The punishment, which made us well, was given to him!

And, we ourselves are healed by means of his wounds. [6]We all have wandered away like sheep. Each of us has gone our own way. But Yahweh has laid upon him the guilt of us all. [7]The One Who Is Always Present says:

"He was beaten down and humiliated. But he didn't even say a word. He was like a lamb being led away to be killed. He was quiet, as a female sheep is silent while her wool is being cut off. He never opened his mouth.

⁸Men took him away violently and unfairly. He died without children to continue his family line.
He was put to death. He was struck down for the sins of his people. ⁹He was supposed to be buried like criminals, even though he had done nothing wrong.
He had never even told a lie! Instead, his death was associated with a rich man."

PRAYER

"Our Lord, mankind hated you. But our souls were drowning in sin and you came along and took them on yourself. Our sins were like spikes in your flesh. The more you suffered, the more our souls were made whole again. The world hated you and you loved us back. Help us be as forgiving to others as you have been to us.

HIS BLOOD

¹⁰Nevertheless, it was Yahweh who decided to crush him; He caused him to suffer. So, the Always-Present One turned his life into a guilt-offering. But he will see his many descendants and live a long life. He will complete the things that Yahweh wants him to do.
¹¹Having suffered many things in his life, he will see the light of life and be satisfied.

The One Who Is Always Present says: "By his knowledge, My righteous Servant will make many people right with God. He will carry away their sins.
¹²For this reason, I will honor him as a great man. He will share in all things with those who are strong.

He willingly gave his life. Yet he was treated like a criminal. But he carried away the sins of many people. And, he interceded for those who had rebelled."

PRAYER

Lord, the world thought you were the sinner and they took you to the cross ~ that heinous instrument of torture. We were there; our sins took you to that cross. Your blood gradually seeped from your body until your heart broke. For us you did this, Lord. For us. Thank you.

Isaiah 53:1-12

WEEK 10

HIS BODY

¹⁸"Come on, let's debate these things. Your sins are red, but they can be as white as snow. Your sins are bright red, but they can be white like wool.

²⁰How horrible it will be for people who call evil things "good," and good things "evil." They think that darkness is light, and light is darkness. They think that sour is sweet, and sweet is sour. ²¹How horrible it will be for people who think they are wise. They think they're so clever. ²²How horrible it will be for people who are "famous" for drinking wine. They are champions at mixing drinks. ²³They receive money to set the guilty free. But they won't allow innocent people to be judged fairly.

¹⁸Yahweh wants to show His mercy to you people. He wants to rise up and comfort you. The Always-Present One is a fair God. And, everyone who waits for His help will be happy....¹³O heavens, sing! O earth, be happy! O mountains, break out in song!
Why? Because Yahweh comforts His people.
He will have compassion upon those who suffer.

PRAYER

Father, it is so popular today to call bad actions good and to look down on good actions. It is so popular today for people to brag about insulting you and doing just the opposite of what would save them from Satan. Today, people play with fire and Satan loves it. Lord, for all the bad we have done, we are so sorry. It cost you your life to bring us back to you. We are so sorry for our sins.

HIS BLOOD

[7]"I will tell about Yahweh's kindnesses. And, I will praise Yahweh for all that He has done for us.
[15]Look down from heaven. Observe us from Your wonderful holy home in heaven.

[5]I said, "Oh no! I will be destroyed. I am not pure. And, I live among people who are not pure.... [14]Nevertheless, the Lord Himself will give you a sign: Look, the virgin will become pregnant. She will give birth to a son, and she will name him 'Immanuel.'

PRAYER

Our holy Father, thank you for your great Plan which began in the Garden of Eden when you promised that one of the descendants of Eve would break Satan's power. For thousands of years you put messages to us in your writings to help us recognize Jesus when he came. And, after those thousands of years, you kept your promise. You did not leave us at the mercy of Satan. You snatched us out of his power at the cross. Thank you.

Isaiah 1:18; Isaiah 5:20-23; Isaiah 6:5a; Isaiah 7:14;

WEEK 11

HIS BODY

[1] Nevertheless, there will be no gloom for those who were once in distress. In the past, God humbled the land of Zebulun and the land of Naphtali. However, in the future, He will make the way of the sea glorious, the land beyond the Jordan River, Galilee of the nations.

[2] Now those people live in darkness, but they will see a great Light. They dwell in a place that is very dark, but Light will shine on them.

[6] Why? Because a special Child will be born to us. God will give us a SON. He will be responsible for leading the people. He will be called:

> "Wonderful"
> "Counselor"
> "Powerful GOD"
> "FATHER of Eternity"
> "Prince of Peace"

[1] A Shoot will grow from the stump of the tree that was cut down. From the family of Jesse, a Branch will bear fruit. [2] The Spirit of the Always-Present One will rest upon him. The Spirit gives him wisdom, understanding, guidance, and power.

PRAYER

Oh God, we thank you for helping us understand what you sacrificed to get us back from Satan. That holy child born in Bethlehem was both Son and God and Father. You sacrificed a part of yourself to free us. How you love us, despite our sins. We do not understand such love. All we can do is thank you.

HIS BLOOD

⁴So, Joseph left Nazareth, a town in Galilee. He went up to the town of Bethlehem in Judea. This was known as David's town. Joseph went there, because he was from the family of David. Joseph was a direct descendant. ⁵Joseph registered with Mary, because she was engaged to marry him. (Mary was now pregnant.)

⁶While they were in Bethlehem, the time came for Mary to have the baby. ⁷She gave birth to her first son and wrapped him in cloths. There were no rooms left in the hotel. So, she laid the baby in a box where livestock are fed.

⁸Some shepherds were spending the night in the fields nearby, watching their flock of sheep. ⁹An angel of the Lord God stood in front of the shepherds. The glory of the Lord shined around them. They were very frightened.

¹⁰The angel said to them, "Don't be afraid, because, listen, I am telling you some good news. It will make all the people very happy. ¹¹This day, your Savior—who is

the Messiah, the Lord—was born in David's town! [12]This is how you will know him: You will find a baby wrapped in cloths and lying in a box where livestock are fed."

[13]Suddenly, a very large group of angels from heaven joined the first angel. They were all praising God:

> [14]"Give glory to God in heaven,
> and, on earth, let there be peace
> among those who please God."

PRAYER

Though angels and dirty shepherds worshipped our Lord when he was born, he went unnoticed by the rest of the world. You left so many messages in your Word to tell us who to look for when you arrived. Herod and the priests knew but hated you. You sacrificed so much to leave heaven and become despised by the world. You came to us in a human body so you could spill your life blood in exchange for our eternal souls. Help us trust you, even when we do not see the signs.

Isaiah 9:1-2, 6-7; Isaiah 11:1-2, Luke 2:4-14

WEEK 12

HIS BODY

¹At that time, you will say: "I praise You, O Yahweh! You were angry with me, but You are not angry with me now! You have comforted me. ²Listen, God is the One who saves me. I trust Him; I'm not afraid. Yahweh, gives me strength and He is my song. He has saved me!" ³You people will receive your salvation with joy. You will get it, just as you would draw water from a well.

⁸But God will destroy Death forever. The Lord Yahweh will wipe away every tear from every face.
God will take away the shame of His people from the entire world. Indeed, Yahweh has spoken!

¹⁸So, Yahweh wants to show His mercy to you people. He wants to rise up and comfort you. The Always-Present One is a fair God. And, everyone who waits for His help will be happy.

PRAYER

Our God, you actually want to show mercy to us despite our sinning against you every day. How do you do it? You even fight our enemy for us, then wipe away our tears. It was done from the cross amidst your agony. Lord, how can we thank you? We worship you.

HIS BLOOD

⁵Then the blind people will see again. Then the deaf will hear. ⁶Then crippled people will jump like a deer. And, those who cannot talk now will shout with joy.
Springs of water will gush forth in the desert. Streams will flow in the dry land. ⁸A road will be there. This highway will be called "The Road to Being Holy."

³This is the voice of a man who calls out: "Prepare in the desert the way for Yahweh. Straighten the road in the dry lands for our God. ⁴Every valley should be raised up. Every mountain and hill should be made flat. The steep ground should be made level. The rugged ground should be made smooth. ⁵Then the splendor of Yahweh will be shown. All mankind together will see it.

The Always-Present One Himself said these things!" ⁸The grass dies, and the flowers fall off. But the Word of our God will live forever."

PRAYER

Lord, you came to us as our king. We should have made the way easy for you, but we did not. Instead, our sins killed you on the cross. You were our king, and did not deserve the cross. But you are able to turn that which was meant for bad into something good. Oh, glorious cross. We will spend the rest of our lives thanking you.

The Lord's Supper: 52 Readings with Prayers

Isaiah 12:1-3; Isaiah 25:8; Isaiah 30:18; Isaiah 35:5-6, 8; Isaiah 40:3-5, 8

WEEK 13

HIS BODY

[1]The Lord Yahweh has put His Spirit in me. This is because Yahweh has anointed me to proclaim the good news to the poor people. He has sent me to comfort those whose hearts are broken. He has sent me to tell the captives that they are free. He has sent me to tell the prisoners that they are released. [2]He has sent me to announce the time when Yahweh will show His kindness.

[1]But now, this is what Yahweh says: "Don't be afraid, because I have redeemed you. I have called you by name, and you belong to Me.

[6]I offered my back to those who beat me. I offered my cheeks to those who pulled my beard. I won't hide my face from them, when they make fun of me and spit on me.

PRAYER

Lord, you went through so much even before they killed you. They beat your back bloody, they pulled hairs out of your beard, they made fun of you, they spit on you, they slapped you. They near killed you before you got to the cross. By your strong will, you survived long enough to be pierced and spill the rest of your blood at the cross as predicted. Such love. Thank you.

HIS BLOOD

[18]And, you will name your walls 'Salvation.' And, you will name your gates 'Praise.' " [19]The sun will no longer be your light during the day. The brightness from the moon will no longer be your light during the night. Instead, Yahweh will be your Light forever. And, your God will be your Beauty. [20]Your sun will never go down again. Your moon will never be dark again.
Why? Because Yahweh will become your Light forever.

It was coming down out of heaven from God. [11]It had God's glory. It was shining like a very valuable jewel—like a crystal-clear jasper stone. [12]The city had a very high wall, with twelve gates and twelve angels at the gates..... The city was 12,000 stadia long. It was 12,000 stadia high and 12,000 stadia wide....[18]The wall was made of jasper. The city was made of pure gold.

PRAYER

Oh God, you made your walls of salvation so high, everyone you save will be safe inside forever. And inside your eternal city, we will need no sun because you will be our light day and night. You treat us like kings even though we are sinners. You wanted to have mercy on us because you love us so. Help us have mercy on others as you have on us.

K. M. Haddad

Isaiah 61:1-2a; Isaiah 43:1; Isaiah 50:6; Isaiah 60:18; Revelation 21:10-11, 16b, 18

WEEK 14

HIS BODY

¹³He is kind and He is merciful. He does not become angry easily. His love is great.

⁴⁶"People will sin against You—everyone sins.... ²⁰Surely there is not a good person on earth, one who always does good and never sins

²²The Always-Present One's love never ends. His mercies never stop. ²³They are fresh every morning. O God, Your faithfulness is great. ²⁴I say to myself, "The Always-Present One is what I've got. Therefore, I have hope, because of Him."

¹⁸There is no God like You. You forgive sin. You overlook the transgressions of God's people. The Always-Present One will not stay angry forever. No, He takes delight in showing mercy. ¹⁹Yahweh will once again have mercy on us. He will conquer our sins. And, You, O God, will throw away all of our sins into the depths of the ocean.

PRAYER

Father, we do not understand your kind of love. We sin against you over and over and you forgive over and over. You never stay angry at us very long. We do something we think you could never forgive but you do.

You delight in us. Lord, help us never take you for granted.

HIS BLOOD

[11]The life of the body is in the blood. And, I have given you special rules for pouring that blood on the altar to cancel your sins. Why? Because it is the blood that cancels the sins!

[26]While they were eating, Jesus took bread and gave thanks. He broke off some of the bread and gave it to his followers. He said, "Take it and eat it. This bread isf my body." [27]Then he took a cup. He gave thanks to God for it and gave it to them. He said, "All of you, drink from it. [28]This is my blood which I am pouring out for many people for the forgiveness of sins.

PRAYER

Our God in heaven, blood is what Satan demanded as the ransom to free mankind from slavery to him. So you gave him what he wanted. Then you tricked him and came back to life. You not only freed us, but you overcame death for us. We have no more fear of death because of your blood. Thank you for what you did for us.

Joel 2:13b; I Kings 8:46; Lamentations 3:22-24; Micah

7:18-19; Leviticus 17:11; Matthew 26:26-28a

K. M. Haddad

WEEK 15

HIS BODY

¹In the beginning was the Word, and the Word was with God, and the Word was deity. ²He was with God in the beginning. ³Through him, everything was made. Without him, nothing which has happened would have happened. ⁴He was the Source of life. That life was the Light for all people. ⁵The Light shines in the darkness; the darkness can never put it out!

¹⁰He was in the world. Through him the world was made, but the people of the world did not acknowledge him. ¹¹He came to what belonged to him, but his own people would not accept him. ¹²But he gave the right to become God's children to those who did accept him, to those who believe in his name. ¹³They were born, not in a human way, or from the natural human desire of men, but born of God.

¹⁴The Word became human and lived among us for a while. We saw his glory, the kind of glory like that of the Father's one and only Son—full of gracious love and truth. ¹⁵John was telling the truth about him. John cried out, "This is the man I talked about: 'The one who is coming behind me has been ahead of me, because he was alive before I was.' "

John saw Jesus coming toward him. John said, "Look, God's Lamb who will take away the world's sin!

PRAYER

Oh God, a part of you materialized for us. You put your words and actions in a body so we could see you in action resisting Satan at every turn. Then the ultimate battle came. Satan had thought he'd won when you died carrying the blame for our sins, but you tricked him and came back to life. For us you did this. We do not know how to thank you enough.

HIS BLOOD

^{5}Jesus answered, "I am telling you the truth: If a person is not born from water and the Spirit, he cannot enter the kingdom of God! ^{6}What has been born from human beings is human. And, what has been born from the Spirit is spiritual. ^{7}Don't be surprised because I said this to you: 'You must be born again.' ^{8}The wind blows wherever it wishes. You hear the sound of it, but you don't know where it comes from or where it is going. It is the same way with everyone who has been born from the Spirit."

^{16}God loved the people of the world so much that He gave up His one and only Son. Every person who commits himself to Jesus will not be destroyed. Instead, that person will have eternal life. ^{17}God did not send His Son into the world to judge it. God sent Jesus, so that the people of the world could be saved through him. ^{18}The person who commits himself to Jesus is not condemned, but the one who does not commit himself to Jesus has already been condemned, because he has not believed in the name of God's one and only Son.

[19]This is the verdict: The Light has come into the world, but people loved the darkness more than they loved the Light, because the things which they were doing were evil. [20]Everyone who does evil hates the Light. He does not come toward the Light. He does not want his evil deeds to be exposed. [21]But the person who is living the truth comes toward the Light. He wants his actions to become clear, because he did them for God.

PRAYER

Oh Lord, you left heaven and came to earth to save us from Satan. You were the light that shone down on people's hypocrisy, acting so holy, but not holy at all. We praise you on Sunday morning and return to whatever we enjoy more on Monday or even Sunday night. Be our light. Without you we flounder through this world. It is so hard to tell good from bad sometimes because Satan makes bad look so wonderful. Continue to be our light and have mercy on us when we fall.

John 1:1-5; 10-14, 29; John 3:5-8, 16-21

WEEK 16

HIS BODY

¹¹"I am the Good Shepherd. The Good Shepherd gives his own life for the sheep. ¹²A man who has been hired is not really a shepherd. The sheep do not belong to him. When he sees a wolf coming, he leaves the sheep and runs away. The wolf catches them and scatters them. ¹³The man doesn't care about the sheep, because he is a hired man.

¹⁴I am the Good Shepherd. I know my followers, and my followers know me, ¹⁵just as the Father knows me and I know my Father. I will give my life for the sheep. ¹⁶But I have some other sheep that are not in this flock. I must lead them, too. They will listen to my voice. Then they will be one flock with one shepherd.

¹⁷Do you know why my Father loves me? Because, I will give my life, so that I may take it back. ¹⁸No one takes it away from me. I am giving it of my own free will. I have the authority to give it, and I have the authority to take it back.

PRAYER

Lord God, we do not understand your kind of undying love which made stronger through your dying. We do not completely understand why Satan accepted his ransom demand and you died for us. We are mere sheep who wander where we should not. Thank you for all you did for us on the cross that day so long ago. Thank you for saving our souls.

HIS BLOOD

^{27}"My soul is very troubled now. What should I say: 'Father, save me from this time of suffering.'? No, the reason I came was for this time. ^{28}Father, bring glory to Your Name!" Then a Voice spoke from heaven, saying, "I have brought glory to it and I will bring glory to it again."

^{29}There was a crowd standing there. They heard the Voice, too. Some of them were saying, "It thundered!" Others were saying, "An angel has spoken to him!" ^{30}Jesus answered, "This Voice did not speak for my sake—but for your sake.

^{31}The time has come for this world to be judged. The time has come for the ruler of this world to be thrown out. ^{32}When I am lifted high above the earth, I will attract everyone to me." ^{33}(Jesus was saying this to show what kind of death he was about to suffer.)

PRAYER

Lord, is so hard to understand the agony Jesus went through, knowing he would have to stand face-to-face with Satan on the cross. Satan smeared Jesus with his own blood and made him a disgrace to mankind. Jesus let him do it, for only then could he be victorious and rise

The Lord's Supper: 52 Readings with Prayers

up the conqueror of Satan and the Savior of our souls. We will thank you for eternity.

John 10:11-18a; John 12:27-33

WEEK 17

HIS BODY

¹Just before the Passover Festival, Jesus knew that his time had come. He must pass from this world to the Father. Jesus loved his own people in the world; he loved them to the very end.

³Jesus knew that the Father had put everything into his hands. He knew that he had come from God and that he was going back to God.

¹After Jesus had said these things, he and his followers went out across Kidron Creek, where there was a garden. They went into the garden. ²Judas (the one who turned against Jesus) also knew the place. Jesus often met there with his followers.

³Then Judas took a group of soldiers and some temple guards who were sent there by the most important priests and Pharisees. They had torches, lanterns, and weapons. ⁴Jesus knew everything which was going to happen to him. He stepped forward and said to them, "Who are you looking for?"

⁵They answered him, "Jesus from Nazareth!"

Jesus said to them, "I am the one."

Judas (the one who turned against Jesus) was standing

there with them. ⁶When Jesus said, "I am the one," they drew back and fell to the ground. ⁷Jesus asked them again, "Who are you looking for?"

They said, "Jesus from Nazareth."

⁸Jesus answered, "I told you that I am the one. Since you are looking for me, let these men go free." ⁹(Jesus said that to make this come true: "I have not lost any of those whom You have given to me.")

¹²The commanding officer, his group of soldiers, and the Jewish temple guards arrested Jesus and tied him up. ¹³They brought him first to Annas who was Caiaphas' father-in-law. Caiaphas was the high priest that year. ¹⁴(He had advised the Jewish leaders that it would be better for one man to die for all of the people.)

PRAYER

Oh Lord, everyone knew how powerful Jesus was or they would not have gone after him with temple guards and Roman soldiers and all their weapons. Each of us has a little bit of those soldiers in us, prepared to fight him to make him weak. Each of us has a little bit of Judas in us, trying to make him what he is not. Each day that we sin, we betray Jesus once again. But he loves us anyway. He forgives us anyway. While in agony on the cross, he forgave us all. We thank you with all our souls.

HIS BLOOD

[19]The high priest asked Jesus about his followers and about his doctrine. [20]Jesus answered him, "I have spoken plainly to the world. I always taught where Jewish people gather—in the synagogues and in the temple courtyard. I have said nothing secretly. [21]Why ask me? Ask those who heard me. Look, they know what I said." [22]When Jesus said this, one of the guards who was standing there struck Jesus. This man asked, "Is that the way to answer the high priest?"

[23]Jesus answered him, "If I said something wrong, show me what it was. If it was good, then why did you hit me?" [24]Then Annas sent Jesus bound to Caiaphas, the high priest.

[33]Pilate went back into the fortress. He called for Jesus and asked him, "Are you the King of the Jews?"

[34]Jesus answered, "Are you saying this on your own, or did someone else tell you this about me?"

[35]Pilate answered, "I am not a Jew, am I? The leading priests and your own people turned you over to me! What have you done?"

[36]Jesus answered, "My kingdom does not come from this world. If it did, my servants would be fighting to keep the Jewish leaders from giving me to you. My kingdom is not from here."

[37]Pilate said to him, "So then, you are a king!"

Jesus answered, "You say that I am a king. The reason I was born, the reason why I have come into the world is to give evidence for the truth. Every person who listens to my voice comes from the truth."

^{38}Pilate asked, "What is truth?"

PRAYER

Lord, we are so confused sometimes on what is truth. Satan lies to us through our friends and tells us to go ahead and sin because God won't really care. Not care? Jesus died in agony for us because he does care. Give us strength, oh God, to read your Words often so we know for sure what truth is, and live in gratitude to you for becoming our King.

John 13:1,3; John 18:1-9; 12-14; 19-24; 33-38

K. M. Haddad

WEEK 18

HIS BODY

¹Then Pilate took Jesus and had them whip him. ²The soldiers made a crown out of thorny branches. They put it on Jesus' head and put a purple robe around him. ³They kept coming up to Jesus and saying, "Hail! O King of the Jews!" They hit him many times.

⁴Pilate went back out and spoke to them, "Look, I am bringing him out to you, so that you will know that I find nothing wrong with him." ⁵Then Jesus came outside. He was wearing the thorny crown and the purple robe. Pilate said to them, "Look at the man!"

⁶When the most important priests and the temple guards saw Jesus, they shouted, "Nail him to a cross! Nail him to a cross!"

Pilate said to them, "You take him and nail him to a cross! I find nothing wrong with him."

⁷But the Jewish leaders answered him, "We have a law. According to the law, he must die, because he made himself God's Son!"

¹³When Pilate heard these words, he brought Jesus outside. Pilate sat down on the judge's seat. He was at a place called "The Stone Pavement." (In the Aramaic language, the name was *Gabbatha*.) ¹⁴It was about

noon on the day before the Passover Festival. Pilate said to the Jewish leaders, "Look, your King!"

PRAYER

Our Father, it is such a shame that those who claimed to honor you despised you, and the outsider ~ Pilot ~ honored you. Things were upside down that day. The religious were lying and making excuses for their creeds while the unreligious pagan saw Jesus as he really was. Father, today more than ever, we declare Jesus our king.

HIS BLOOD

^{15}They yelled, "Take him away! Take him away! Nail him to a cross!"

Pilate said to them, "Should I nail your King to a cross?"

The most important priests answered, "The only king we have is Caesar!" ^{16}Then Pilate turned Jesus over to them to be nailed to the cross. So they took hold of Jesus.

^{17}Jesus was carrying his own cross. He went out to the place which was called Skull Place. (In Aramaic, it is named Golgotha.)

^{18}This is where they nailed him to the cross, along with two other men. Jesus' cross was between the crosses of the other two men.

[19]Pilate made a sign and put it on Jesus' cross. It read:

> "JESUS FROM NAZARETH,
> THE KING OF THE JEWS."

[20]Many Jewish people read this sign. This place where Jesus was crucified was near the city of Jerusalem. The sign was written in Aramaic, in Latin, and in Greek. [21]The most important Jewish priests kept saying to Pilate, "Don't write: 'The King of the Jews'! Instead, you should write: 'This man said, "I am the King of the Jews." ' "

[22]Pilate answered, "What I have written stays written!"

PRAYER

Lord, help us see your truths as clearly as Pilot did that day. Keep us away from all the confusing creeds and synods and councils that decide for us what to believe. Keep us simple in our belief with one truth ~ that Jesus truly was the Son of God.

John 19:1-7; 13-22

WEEK 19

HIS BODY

²³After the soldiers had nailed Jesus to the cross, they took his clothes and divided them into four parts—one for each soldier, but the robe remained. This robe was seamless—completely made of one piece of woven cloth. ²⁴They said to one another, "Let's not tear it. Let's gamble for it, to see who will get it!" This happened to make this Scripture come true:

> "They divided my clothes among themselves.
> They gambled for my clothing."

That is what the soldiers did.

²⁵Jesus' mother, his mother's sister, Mary the wife of Clopas, and Mary from the town of Magdala stood near the cross. ²⁶Jesus saw his mother and the follower whom he loved standing there. He said to his mother, "Woman, look at your son." ²⁷Then Jesus said to that follower, "Look at your mother." From that moment on, that follower accepted Mary as his own mother.

PRAYER

Lord, even from the agony of the cross you thought of others. You could see in the crowd that day which ones risked being crucified themselves in order to stay near you to the end. Today, help us not forsake the cross on which he died. Let the cross be ever our glory.

HIS BLOOD

²⁸After this, when Jesus knew that everything was finished, he said this to make the Scripture come true: "I am thirsty." ²⁹There was a jar full of sour wine nearby. So they soaked a sponge in it and put it on a long stick. Then they brought this to Jesus' mouth. ³⁰After Jesus drank some of it, he said, "It is finished!" Then he bowed his head and died.

³²The soldiers came to the first man and broke his legs, and then to the other man who had been nailed to a cross, too. ³³But when they came to Jesus, they saw that Jesus was already dead. They did not break his legs, ³⁴but one of the soldiers did plunge his spear into Jesus' side. Immediately, blood and water flowed out. ³⁵The person who saw it has given proof. His testimony is true. You know he is speaking the truth. You must believe, too. ³⁶These things happened to make this Scripture come true:

> "Not one of his bones will be broken."

³⁷Another Scripture says:

> "They will look upon the one they pierced."

PRAYER

Fulfilled. Jesus had now fulfilled all the prophecies about his death. And he had fulfilled all the Law of Moses perfectly. So now it was ready to pass away in favor of Jesus' law of grace. With his blood now drained from his body and a great cry of agony, he died for us. But it was also a cry of triumph. How Jesus loved us to give his life in our place. How he loved us. Thank you.

John 19:23-30; John 19:32-38

K. M. Haddad

WEEK 20

HIS BODY

[1]It was very early on Sunday morning. It was still dark. Mary (the one from Magdala) came to the tomb. She saw the stone moved away from the tomb.

[2]Then she ran and came to Simon Peter and the other follower whom Jesus loved. She said to them, "They have taken away the Lord Jesus from the tomb! We don't know where they put him!"

[3]Then Peter and the other follower left. They went to the tomb. [4]Both of them were running, but the other follower outran Peter. He arrived at the tomb first. [5]He bent down and saw the sheets lying there, but he did not go inside. [6]Then Simon Peter came, following. Peter went into the tomb. He also saw the sheets lying there. [7]But the handkerchief which had been on Jesus' face was not lying with the sheets. Instead, it was all alone, in one place—folded up. [8]Then the other follower, who had come to the tomb first, also went in. He saw and he believed. [9](They did not yet know the Scripture which said that Jesus must rise from death.) [10]The two followers went back home.

PRAYER

Isn't that the way we are, oh God? We only stay around to hear half the story? Mary saw the empty tomb and decided Jesus' body had been stolen. When Peter went inside the tomb, did he believe Jesus had been beheaded and his body abused further? Then John went in and instantly he believed. How slow we are, Lord, to read your Word and accept it as it is instead of bringing in our own conclusions. A simple empty tomb. A tomb that meant victory over death. Help us understand more so we may thank you more.

HIS BLOOD

[11]Mary was standing outside the tomb, crying. While she was crying, she bent down to look into the tomb. [12]She saw two angels dressed in white clothes. They were seated where Jesus' body had been lying—one at the head and one at the foot. [13]They asked her, "Woman, why are you crying?"

She answered them, "They took my Lord away! I don't know where they put him!" [14]After she said this, she turned around. She saw Jesus standing there, but she didn't know that it was Jesus.

[15]Jesus said to her, "Woman, why are you crying? Who are you looking for?"

Thinking that Jesus was the gardener, she said to him, "Mister, if you carried him off, tell me where you put him and I will take him away."

[16]Jesus said to her, "Mary!"

She turned and said to Jesus in Aramaic, "Rabboni!" (This word means "My Teacher!")

[17] Jesus said to her, "Don't cling to me; I have not yet gone up to the Father. Go to my brothers and tell them this: 'I am going up to my Father and your Father, to my God and to your God.' " [18] Mary (the one from Magdala) went and told the followers, "I have seen the Lord Jesus!" She told them that he had talked with her.

PRAYER

Lord, Mary was so confused. In her grief she was confused. Sometimes when we sin and grieve over what we did, we become confused. We forget that you forgive all sins. We stay in our sins until we remember with clarity you died to save us from Satan. You died and lived again, and so shall we someday. Thank you for giving us clarity and saving our souls.

John 20:1-18

WEEK 21

HIS BODY

[19]It was late that same Sunday. The doors were locked where the followers were gathered. They were afraid of the Jewish leaders. Jesus came and stood in the middle of them. He said to them, "Peace be to you!" [20]After Jesus said this, he showed them his hands and his side. When the followers saw the Lord Jesus, they were happy. [21]Then Jesus said to them again, "Peace to you. I am sending you just as the Father has sent me." [22]After Jesus said this, he breathed on them and said to them, "Receive the Holy Spirit! [23]If you say some people are forgiven, then they are forgiven. But, if you say that the sins of some people are not forgiven, then they are not forgiven."

[24]Thomas (the one called "The Twin") was one of the twelve apostles. He was not with them when Jesus came. [25]The other followers continued to tell Thomas, "We have seen the Lord Jesus!"

Thomas said to them, "I will never believe it, unless I see the marks of the nails in his hands, unless I put my finger into the marks of the nails, unless I put my hand into his side!"

PRAYER

Lord, it is so easy for us today to say, "Oh, yes, Jesus came out of his grave alive again." Help us examine our hearts. Do we say it just because everyone else does? If we were born among, Buddhists, Hindus, Muslims or atheists, would we say it? Have we studied the prophecies Jesus fulfilled enough to believe it, even when no one else does? Help us not condemn Thomas too easily. Help us study your Word enough that we really and truly believe Jesus came back to life after giving his body over to be crucified. Thank you for what he did to save us from hell. We worship you.

HIS BLOOD

^{26}A week later, Jesus' followers were inside again. Thomas was with them, too. The doors were locked, but Jesus came and stood in the middle of them and said, "Peace be to you!" ^{27}Then Jesus said to Thomas, "Look at my hands! Put your finger here. Bring your hand here and put it in my side. Stop doubting and start believing!"

^{28}Thomas answered Jesus, "My Lord and my God!"

^{29}Jesus said to him, "You have believed, because you have seen me. The happy ones are those who have not seen me and yet who believe."

PRAYER

Lord, all the other apostles disbelieved the women when they said Jesus was alive again. The apostles were all like Thomas. But he was the first to call Jesus God.

Grant us strength for our belief. Help our unbelief.
Jesus did truly spill his blood in exchange for our souls.
Make us strong in our belief.

John 20:19-21

WEEK 22

HIS BODY

¹⁶God loved the people of the world so much that He gave up His one and only Son. Every person who commits himself to Jesus will not be destroyed. Instead, that person will have eternal life.

⁵³Jesus said to them, "I am telling you the truth: If you don't eat my flesh and you don't drink my blood, you do not have life in you! ⁵⁴The person who eats my flesh and drinks my blood has eternal life. I will raise him from death on the last day. ⁵⁵My flesh is real food and my blood is real drink. ⁵⁶The person who eats my flesh and drinks my blood stays in me and I stay in him.

⁷God is in the light. We should also live in light. If we live in the light, then we have a relationship of sharing with each other, and the blood of Jesus, God's Son, continues to cleanse us from all sin. ⁸Since the beginning, the Devil has been sinning. The person who continues to sin belongs to the Devil. Why did the Son of God appear? To destroy the Devil's works.

PRAYER

Oh, thank you, Lord God. Even though we continue to sin every day of our lives, your blood continues to cleanse us from all those sins. Thank you for destroying the works of Satan. Thank you for continuing to keep us safe from the enemy of our souls. Thank you for being the lover of our souls.

HIS BLOOD

[18]You know the worthless kind of life you got from your forefathers. You were not purchased from this with something that doesn't last, like silver or gold. [19]No, it was with the precious blood of Christ, like that of a perfect lamb; nothing is wrong with it. [20]Before the world was made, God chose Christ; but now, in the last times, Christ has appeared for your sake. [21]Through Christ, you believe in God. God raised Christ from death and gave glory to him. Now your faith and hope can be toward God.

[24]In his body he carried our sins on the wooden cross. He wants us to quit sinning and live right. His wounds were used to heal us.

PRAYER

Lord, on the cross that day, your wounds touched our souls and healed us of our sins. You took the blackness of our sins onto yourself, died with them, and buried them for good. When you arose, it was only you and your goodness that returned. We cannot thank you enough, Lord, for all you did to save us from Satan, our enemy, and declare us your children.

K. M. Haddad

John 3:16; John 6:53-56; I John 1:7; I John 3:8; I Peter 1:18-21; I Peter 2:24

WEEK 23

HIS BODY

[14]The time came for them to eat the Passover meal. Jesus and the apostles were sitting around the table. [15]Jesus said to them, "I wanted very much to eat this Passover meal with you before I die. [16]I tell you, I will never eat another Passover meal until it is given its true meaning in the kingdom of God."

[17]Then Jesus took a cup. He gave thanks to God for it. Then he said, "Take this cup and give it to everyone here. [18]I tell you, I will never drink from the fruit of the vine again until God's kingdom comes."

[19]Then Jesus took bread and gave thanks. He broke off some of the bread and gave it to them. Then he said, "This bread is my body which I am giving for you. Eat this to remember me." [20]In the same way, after supper, Jesus took a cup and said, "This cup is God's new covenant sealed by my blood, which is being poured out for you."

PRAYER

Lord, How hard was it for the apostles to eat a substitute for Jesus body while he was still with them in the flesh? Did Jesus have to make them do it? But today, we thank you for allowing us to eat the bread with you in spirit. Today we thank you for the reminder of what you did for us. His apostles did not want him to die. But today we understand why you did and reach out to you with our hearts to say thank you.

HIS BLOOD

$^{39\text{-}40}$Jesus went out of Jerusalem to Olive Mountain. His followers went with him. (Jesus often went there.) He said to his followers, "Pray for strength against temptation."

^{41}Then Jesus went off about 50 yards away from them. He kneeled down and began to pray, ^{42}"Father, if it is in Your plan, then take this cup of suffering away from me. Nevertheless, what You want is more important than what I want." ^{43}Then an angel from heaven appeared. The angel was sent to help Jesus be stronger. ^{44}Jesus was full of deep concern; he struggled hard in prayer. Sweat dripped from his face to the ground as though he were bleeding.

PRAYER

Oh, how Jesus dreaded becoming every murderer, every rapist, every torturer, every thief, every liar, every abuser who ever walked the earth. How he dreaded becoming what he hated. We did that to him with our sins. But now he says, "It's all gone. I have washed you clean with my blood. How can we thank you enough?

The Lord's Supper: 52 Readings with Prayers

Luke 22:14-20; 39-44

WEEK 24

HIS BODY

⁵⁴They seized Jesus and took him away. They brought him into the high priest's house.

⁶³⁻⁶⁴Some men were guarding Jesus. This is the way they made fun of Jesus: They covered his eyes, so that he couldn't see them. Then they hit him and said, "Prophesy for us! Let God tell you which one of us hit you!" ⁶⁵The men were saying many other terrible things to Jesus.

PRAYER

How many lies about you do people believe today just as the soldiers did that terrible night before your death? The soldiers believed they could beat on you, spit on you, make fun of you with no consequences. Today people still beat on Christianity and laugh that they get by with it. Lord, when people treat us that way for being Christians, help us be as patient with them as you were. Thank you for the privilege of being persecuted for you. Thank you for, not only enduring torture for us, but for dying in our place.

HIS BLOOD

⁶⁶When morning came, the elders of the people, the most important priests, and the teachers of the law all

came together. They led Jesus away to their Jewish Council. [67]They said, "Since you claim that you are the Messiah, tell us that you are!"

Jesus said to them, "If I were to tell you that I am the Messiah, you would never believe it. [68]And if I were to ask you, you wouldn't answer. [69]But I will sit at the right side of God's throne from now on!"

[70]They all asked, "So, are you the Son of God!?"

Jesus said to them, "Yes, you are the ones who said it."

[71]They said, "Why do we need witnesses now!? We ourselves just heard it from his own lips!

PRAYER

Lord, you made your enemies say it. They wanted you to say you were the Son of God, but you wanted them to form those words themselves. They knew who you were, and so their lips finally formed the words they hated ~ You are the Son of God. You were always in charge. You still are today. So, no matter how bad our world may become, help us remember you are always in charge. Thank you for laying down on your cross as though it was the altar of the world, and raising us on high with you.

Luke 22:54,63-71

WEEK 25

HIS BODY

¹Then the whole group stood up and led Jesus to Pilate. ²They began to accuse Jesus. They said, "We caught this man telling things which were confusing our people. He says we should stop paying taxes to Caesar. He calls himself the Messiah, a king."

³Pilate asked Jesus, "Are you the King of the Jews?"

Jesus answered him, "Yes, you are the one who says it."

⁴Pilate said to the most important priests and to the crowds, "I find nothing wrong with this man."

⁵They said again and again, "But Jesus is making trouble with the people! He teaches all over Judea. He began in Galilee, and now he is here!"

¹³Pilate called everyone together. He called the most important priests, the Jewish leaders, and the people. ¹⁴He said to them, "You brought this man Jesus to me. You said he was making trouble among the people. But, listen, I judged him in front of all of you. I found no criminal charge in him. Jesus is not guilty of the things you are claiming against him. ¹⁵Herod Antipas found nothing wrong with him, either; he sent him back to us. Look, Jesus has done no criminal act. He shouldn't be

killed. [16]So, after I give him some punishment, I will let him go free."

PRAYER

Lord, help us never lie and falsely accuse someone in order to protect our position. It took an outsider ~ Pilate ~ to see what those religious leaders were doing. Oh, the sins we commit when trying to make ourselves more important than others. Father, help us see ourselves as you do. Help us be willing to bow before others and wash their feet. We thank you for your example of how to live and how to die.

HIS BLOOD

[18]But all of the people yelled, "Kill him! Set Barabbas free for us!" [19](Barabbas was a man who was thrown into prison because of a riot which took place in the city, and for murder.)

[20]Pilate really wanted to let Jesus go free. So, Pilate appealed to them again. [21]But they yelled again, "Kill him! Nail him to a cross!"

[22]A third time, Pilate said to them, "Why? What crime has Jesus done!? He is not guilty. I can find no reason to kill him. So, I will set him free, after I give him some punishment."

[23]But the people continued to yell. They demanded that Jesus be executed on a cross. Their yelling became so

loud that [24]Pilate decided to give them what they wanted. The people wanted Barabbas to go free. [25](Barabbas was the man who had been thrown into jail because of a riot. He was a murderer.) Pilate let Barabbas go free, but Pilate gave them Jesus to be executed. This is what the people wanted.

PRAYER

Oh, Father, it was our sins that took Jesus to the cross that day. We and our pride and our selfishness were in that crowd. Help us learn to stand apart from the crowd, even if they turn on us next. Help us be more like you. We offer you our lives and our souls.

Luke 23:3-5; 13-25

WEEK 26

HIS BODY

²⁶The soldiers led Jesus away to be killed. At that same time, there was a man coming into the city from the fields. His name was Simon. He was from the city of Cyrene. The soldiers forced him to carry Jesus' cross and to walk behind Jesus.

²⁷A very large crowd was following Jesus. Some of the women were crying and wailing for Jesus. ²⁸Jesus turned and said to the women, "Women of Jerusalem, don't cry for me—cry for yourselves and also for your children! ²⁹Listen, the time is coming when people will say, 'Happy are the women who cannot have babies! Happy are the women who have never had children, who have never nursed children.' ³⁰Then the people will begin to say to the mountains, 'Fall on us!' The people will say to the hills, 'Cover us!' ³¹If people do things like this now when life is good, what will happen when bad times come?"

³²⁻³³There were also two criminals led out with Jesus. Jesus and the two criminals were led to a place where they would be killed. The people called this place "The Skull." There some men nailed Jesus to his cross. They also nailed the criminals to their crosses; Jesus' cross was between the crosses of the two criminals. ³⁴Jesus said, "Father, forgive these people. They don't know what they are doing."

PRAYER

Lord, thank you for all you went through in order to grab our souls out of the clutches of Satan and put us in the safety of your fold. We cannot fully comprehend all you went through, but we will spend the rest of our lives trying to understand better and thanking you.

HIS BLOOD

The soldiers gambled to see who would get Jesus' clothes.

[35] The people stood there watching. The Jewish leaders were laughing at Jesus. They said, "Since he is 'God's chosen one', the Messiah, let him save himself! He saved other people, didn't he!?"

[36] Even the soldiers made fun of him. They came to Jesus and offered him some sour wine. [37] The soldiers said, "If you are the King of the Jews, save yourself!"

[38] At the top of the cross these words were written:

"THIS IS THE KING OF THE JEWS."

PRAYER

Oh Lord, we are the ones who should have been on the cross that day. We are the ones who should have had our hands and feet stabbed by spikes and left to hang in torture until our blood drained from our body. How can we thank you for taking our place? We will spend eternity trying.

Luke 23:26-38

WEEK 27

HIS BODY

⁴⁴It was about noon, but the whole area became dark until three o'clock in the afternoon. ⁴⁵There was no sun! The curtain hanging between the holy place and the most holy place in the temple was torn right down the middle. ⁴⁶Jesus shouted, "Father, I put my spirit into Your hands." After Jesus said this, he died.

⁴⁷The Roman army officer saw what happened. He was giving glory to God, saying, "This man was truly righteous!"

⁴⁸Many people had come out of the city to see this event. When the people saw it, they felt deep sorrow and left. ⁴⁹The people who were close friends of Jesus were there. Also, there were some women who had followed Jesus from Galilee. They all stood far away from the cross to watch.

PRAYER

Our God in heaven. What Jesus went through for us is indescribable and beyond our understanding. The last three dark hours of Jesus' life was wrung out of him by a merciless crowd. Yet, you are merciful even to the merciless. Jesus could have stopped it all and returned to heaven early. But he saw it through ~ wringing us out of the clutches of Satan. Mighty victory! Thank you.

HIS BLOOD

⁵⁰⁻⁵¹There was a man from Arimathea, a Judean town. His name was Joseph. He was a good, righteous man. He was earnestly looking for the kingdom of God. Joseph was a member of the Jewish Council, but he did not vote when the priests decided to kill Jesus. ⁵²Joseph went to Pilate to ask for the body of Jesus. ⁵³So, Joseph took the body down from the cross and wrapped it in a linen cloth. Then he put Jesus' body into a cave which was cut out of solid rock. This tomb had never been used before. ⁵⁴This was late on a Friday afternoon. (When the sun went down, the sabbath day would begin.)

⁵⁵The women who had come from Galilee with Jesus followed Joseph. They observed the tomb. Inside, they saw where the body of Jesus was placed. ⁵⁶Then the women left to prepare some fragrant things to put on Jesus' body.

They rested on the sabbath day, according to God's command.

PRAYER

Our God, what was it like for them to bury their Lord, believing all hope was gone? What was it like for a few brave ones to have a secret funeral in the darkness of that tomb? What was it like for his apostles to go into hiding and mourn the death of their Savior and their dreams? Thank you for seeing it through. Help us, when things seem to wrong, to realize you are always in control and you have greater plans than we ever dreamed of. You turned the blood of Jesus into a glorious victory for us. How can we thank you enough?

Luke 23:44-56

WEEK 28

HIS BODY

¹Very early on Sunday morning, the women came to the tomb. They brought the fragrant things they had prepared. ²But the women found that the rock was rolled away from the tomb. ³They went in, but they didn't find the Lord Jesus' body.

⁴While they were wondering about it, suddenly, two angels stood beside them in shining clothes. ⁵The women were frightened; they bowed their heads down to the ground. The two angels said to the women, "Why are you looking here for a living person!? This is a place for dead people! ⁶Jesus is not here. He has risen from death! Do you remember what he said to you while he was still in Galilee? ⁷Jesus said that he must be handed over to evil men, be killed on a cross, and rise from death on the third day." ⁸Then the women remembered Jesus' words.

PRAYER

Our God, you had to send special messengers to tell the women what Jesus had been saying all along was true: He was going to die and he was going to come back to life. We read great things in the Bible and only half believe them when the time comes. Yes, Jesus' body was gone. That was only because Jesus was back in that body. Wake us up, Lord, and help us believe you with a stronger faith. And, Lord, thank you for your example.

HIS BLOOD

⁹The women left the tomb and went to the eleven apostles and to all the other followers. The women told them everything which had occurred at the tomb.

¹⁰The women were: Mary of Magdala, Joanna, Mary (the mother of James), and some other women. These women were telling the apostles everything that had happened. ¹¹But the men didn't believe what the women said. It sounded crazy.

¹²However, Peter got up and ran to the tomb. He bent down and looked in, but the only things he saw were the grave clothes. Peter went off by himself, wondering about what had taken place.

PRAYER

Father in heaven, our faith is so weak. If Jesus' closest friends didn't believe he was back in his body, do we really and truly believe that, when we die, we will have the likeness of Jesus' glorious body? Or do we hang back from dying, hang back from stepping into your glorious world? Jesus proved to us by returning to life that we will too. God, we believe. Help our unbelief.

Luke 24:1-12

WEEK 29

HIS BODY

³⁶While they were discussing these things, Jesus himself stood among them. He said to them, "Peace to you."

³⁷They began to be filled with fear. They were terrified. They thought they were seeing a ghost. ³⁸But Jesus asked them, "Why are you so disturbed!? Why do you doubt what you see!? ³⁹Look at my hands and my feet. It is really me! Touch me. You can see that I have a living body; a ghost doesn't have a body like this."

⁴⁰After Jesus told them this, he showed them the holes in his hands and feet. ⁴¹They were amazed but very, very happy to see that he was alive. They still couldn't believe it. So, Jesus asked them, "Do you have any food here?" ⁴²They gave him a piece of cooked fish. ⁴³While they watched, Jesus took it and ate it.

⁴⁴Jesus said to them, "Do you remember when I was with you before? I said that everything written about me must come true—everything written in the law of Moses, the books of the prophets, and the Psalms."

PRAYER

Father, our faith is so weak. The apostles thought they were strong, but they weren't. Help us face our faith today and ask ourselves, "If I was informed I would die within a month, would I panic or would I praise God?" Do we truly believe what Jesus said? Help us examine our faith."

HIS BLOOD

⁴⁵Then Jesus explained the Scriptures. He helped them to understand the things which had been written about him. ⁴⁶Then Jesus said to them, "Thus it is written that the Messiah would be killed and come back to life from death on the third day. ⁴⁷⁻⁴⁸You saw these things happen.

You must go and tell all nations that their sins can be forgiven. Tell them that they must change their hearts. You must start from Jerusalem and proclaim these things with my authority. ⁴⁹Listen, I am sending my Father's promise upon you. But you must stay in Jerusalem until you are clothed with that power from heaven."

⁵⁰Jesus led them out of Jerusalem, almost to the town of Bethany. He raised his hands and blessed them. ⁵¹While Jesus was blessing them, he was separated from them and carried up into heaven.

PRAYER

Oh, God. You not only returned to your body, but you let them watch you rise up to the sky. You gave this account in your Word to help our faith. We believe we will die and return to you some day. Help our unbelief.

Luke 24:36-48

WEEK 30

HIS BODY

¹⁷When evening came, Jesus sat down at the table with his twelve followers.

²²While they were eating, Jesus took bread and gave thanks to God. He broke off some of it and gave it to them. He said, "Take it. This bread is my body." ²³⁻²⁴Then he took a cup. He gave thanks to God for it and gave it to them. He said, "All of you, drink from it. This is my blood for the covenant. It is being poured out for many people. ²⁵I am telling you the truth: I will never drink the fruit of the vine again, until the day when I drink it new in the kingdom of God."

²⁶Then they sang a song of praise and went out to Olive Mountain.

PRAYER

Lord, how the hearts of the apostles must have been breaking when told to eat Jesus' flesh and drink his blood. They wanted Jesus with them forever. They did not understand Jesus had to die so they could do just that ~ live with him forever. Help us face our own death in the same way ~ knowing we have to die in order to see Jesus and live with him forever. Thank you for willingly going through all that agony to make our glorious eternity with you possible.

HIS BLOOD

⁷During Jesus' human life, he offered prayers to God. With strong cries and tears, Jesus asked God to save him from death.

³²Then they went to a place called Gethsemane. Jesus said to his followers, "Sit here while I go pray."

³³He took Peter, James, and John along with him. He began to feel very sad and depressed. ³⁴Then he said to them, "My soul is full of sorrow; I am going to die. Stay here and be watchful." ³⁵Then Jesus went ahead a short distance and fell down on the ground. He was praying that, if possible, this time might pass away from him. ³⁶He continued to pray, "Father, dear Father, all things are possible for You. Take this cup of suffering away from me, but what You want is more important than what I want."

³⁷Then Jesus came and found them sleeping. He said to Peter, "Are you asleep, Simon? Were you not strong enough to watch one hour? ³⁸Watch and pray for strength against yielding to temptation. The spirit is willing, but the body is weak."

³⁹Again Jesus went away. He prayed the same prayer. ⁴⁰Once more, Jesus came and found them sleeping. Their eyes were very tired. The men didn't know what to say to him. ⁴¹Jesus came back the third time and said to them, "Are you still sleeping and resting? That's enough! The time has come. Listen! I am being handed over into

the hands of sinful men. ⁴²Get up, we must go. Look! The one who turned against me is near!"

PRAYER

Lord God, the apostles had to have heard him when he was calling out in agony. Did they will themselves not to hear him because of their own grief over losing him? Jesus was about to be tortured by both the Romans and Satan. He was about to let his body be abused, his blood drained from that body, and tortured by Satan. Lord, is our faith in you as weak as the apostles that night? Thank you for forgiving our weaknesses. We love you.

Mark 14:17, 22-26; Hebrews 5:7a; Mark 32-42-50

WEEK 31

HIS BODY

⁴³And, immediately, while Jesus was still speaking, Judas, one of the twelve apostles, came. There was a crowd with him. They had sticks and swords. They had come from the most important priests, the teachers of the law, and the Jewish elders. ⁴⁴Judas had given them a signal: "Arrest the man whom I kiss; it's him! Lead him away carefully." ⁴⁵Immediately Judas came to Jesus and said to him, "Rabbi!" Then Judas kissed him.

⁴⁶Then they reached out and grabbed Jesus. ⁴⁷One of the men standing nearby pulled out his sword. He struck the high priest's servant, cutting off his ear.

⁴⁸Jesus asked them, "Why did you come out here with swords and sticks? Do you think I am a criminal? ⁴⁹I was teaching in the temple courtyard every day. I was with you. You did not arrest me there. No, this occurred to make the Scriptures come true." ⁵⁰Then all of Jesus' followers left him. They ran away.

⁵³They brought Jesus to the high priest. All of the important priests, the teachers of the law, and the Jewish elders came together

⁵⁵The most important priests and the whole Jewish Council wanted to find some men who would give evidence against Jesus, so that they could kill him. But,

they did not find any real proof. ⁵⁶Many people were telling lies against Jesus, but their testimony did not match. ⁵⁷Some men stood up and told this lie against Jesus: ⁵⁸"We heard this man say: 'I will destroy this temple sanctuary built by men and build another one in three days—without human hands!' " ⁵⁹Their testimony still did not agree. ⁶⁰The high priest stood up in the center and asked Jesus, "Aren't you going to answer? What they are saying against you—is it true?" ⁶¹Jesus continued to be silent; he gave no answers.

PRAYER

Father, when people lie about us, help us remain silent. They already have their minds made up about us. Help us live more like Jesus so that liars are not believed. What those who hated Jesus were about to do was to destroy him, but it only made him stronger. Thank you for offering that body to mankind so you could save us.

HIS BLOOD

Again, the high priest asked Jesus, "Are you the Messiah, the Son of the Blessed One?"

⁶²Jesus said, "I am!

'You people will see the Son of Man sitting at the right side of God. He will be coming with the clouds of the sky!' "

⁶³Then the high priest ripped his own clothes. He said,

"Why do we need any more witnesses? ^{64}You heard the evil thing that Jesus said! How does it look to you?"

They all condemned him, saying, "He is guilty! He should be killed!" ^{65}Some of them began to spit on Jesus. They covered his face and hit him with their fists. They said to him, "Prophesy!" And when the guards took charge of him, they started beating up on him.

PRAYER

Lord, sometimes we pretend to be so holy when all we are doing to defending our egos. We pretend righteous indignation over some wrong, but only because our friends do. When Jesus finally spoke, it was to tell them more than they wanted to know. They were after Jesus' blood, and they got it. Still, through it all, Jesus was willing to forgive. Thank you for Jesus' life and his death.

Mark 14:43-50, 53-65

K. M. Haddad

WEEK 32

HIS BODY

¹It was early in the morning. The most important priests, the teachers of the law, and the Jewish elders—the whole council—were soon ready. They tied up Jesus, took him, and gave him to Pilate. ²Pilate asked Jesus, "Are you the king of the Jews?"

Jesus answered, "Yes." ³Some important priests were there accusing Jesus of many things. ⁴Again, Pilate asked him, "Won't you say anything? Look at how many charges they are bringing against you!"

⁵But Jesus gave no answers. Pilate was surprised.

⁶At each Passover Feast, Pilate always set one prisoner free, the one whom the people wanted. ⁷A man named Barabbas was arrested with some rebels. They had committed murder during a riot. ⁸The crowd came up and began to ask Pilate to do the same thing as he always did for them.

PRAYER

Lord, when the people who hated Jesus saw they were about to lose, they came up with a new plan to kill him. They knew who he was and refused to believe in him. How submissive are we, Lord? Sometimes we come up with new plans to do wrong and make that wrong look so right. Kill our egos, Lord, and help us live and act more like Jesus, our strong Savior.

HIS BLOOD

^{9}Pilate answered them, "Do you want me to release the King of the Jews for you?" ^{10}(Pilate knew the leading priests had turned Jesus over to him because they were jealous of Jesus.)

^{11}The most important priests made the people excited. They wanted Pilate to set Barabbas free for them, instead of Jesus.

^{12}Again Pilate asked them, "What do you want me to do with Jesus, the one you call 'King of the Jews'?"

^{13}They yelled again, "Nail him to a cross!"

^{14}Pilate said to them, "Why? What crime has Jesus done?"

But they continued to yell even more, "Nail him to a cross!"

^{15}Pilate wanted to please the people. So, he set Barabbas free for them. After beating Jesus with whips, Pilate handed him over to be nailed to the cross.

PRAYER

Our Father, do we give in to the people around us in order to keep their friendship and approval? Help us see ourselves and strive to do better. Help us be willing to die with Christ.

Mark 15:1-15

WEEK 33

HIS BODY

¹⁶The soldiers took Jesus inside the courtyard of the Roman fortress. The whole group gathered around Jesus. ¹⁷They dressed him with a purple robe. They used thorny branches to make a crown. ¹⁸Then they began to salute Jesus, saying, "Hail, O King of the Jews!" ¹⁹They hit Jesus many times on the head with a stick and they were spitting on him. They kneeled down and acted as though they were worshiping him. ²⁰When they finished making fun of him, they took off the purple robe and dressed him with his own clothes. Then they led him away to nail him to the cross.

²¹There was a man coming into the city from the fields. He was Simon, from the city of Cyrene. (He was the father of Alexander and Rufus.)ᶜ They forced him to carry the cross of Jesus.

²²They brought Jesus to the place of Golgotha. (This means "The Place of the Skull.") ²³They gave him some wine mixed with myrrh, but Jesus didn't drink it. ²⁴Then they nailed him to the cross. The soldiers gambled to see who would get Jesus' clothes. ²⁵It was about nine o'clock in the morning when they nailed Jesus to the cross. ²⁶At the top of the cross, they nailed up a sign of his "crime" with these words:

"THE KING OF THE JEWS."

PRAYER

Lord God, Jesus was so weak after all the terrible things they did to him during the night. So many often died after scourging. His mighty will kept him alive long enough he could fulfill the final prophecies ~ so they could pierce him. Lord, we sin every day and, in a sense, we drive those spikes into his body once again. We are so ashamed, and in our shame, we look to you and say thank you.

HIS BLOOD

[27] Along with Jesus, two criminals were nailed to crosses. One was at his right. And, the other was on his left. [29] The people who were passing by shook their heads and said terrible things to Jesus. They said, "Bah! You were the one who was going to destroy the temple sanctuary and build it again in three days!? [30] Save yourself! Come on down from the cross!"

[31] The most important priests, together with the teachers of the law, made fun of Jesus to each other in the same way. They continued to say, "He saved other people, but he cannot save himself! [32] He is the King of Israel, the Messiah; let him come down from the cross now, so that we can see and believe!"

PRAYER

Oh, Father, help us never to gloat at the downfall of someone else. How arrogant the so-called religious people acted as they got rid of their competition. They were blood-thirsty and got their wish. But in destroying Jesus, they destroyed themselves. By killing him, they made it possible for him to come back to life. Thank you, Jesus, for staying on the cross so some day you could wash us in your blood and make our souls white as snow.

Mark 15:16-32

WEEK 34

HIS BODY

³³From noon until three o'clock in the afternoon, there was darkness over the entire land. ³⁴About three o'clock, Jesus cried out loudly, *"Eloi, Eloi, lama sa-bak-tha-ni?"* (This means: "My God, my God, why did You abandon me?")

³⁵Some of the men standing there heard this. They said, "Look! He is calling Elijah." ³⁶Someone ran and soaked a sponge in some sour wine. Then he put it on the end of a long stick and gave Jesus a drink. Someone said, "Leave him alone! Let us see if Elijah will come down for him!"

³⁷Jesus gave out a loud cry and died. ³⁸The curtain in the temple sanctuary was split from the top to the bottom into two parts.

PRAYER

We realize Jesus had to be separated from you, Father, because he had become every sinner in the world from the creation of mankind. The load was heavy and the price he paid terrible, and he dreaded that moment all his life: Being separated from God the Father with no hope. Then he cried, "It is fulfilled." He knew he had done everything necessary to take our punishment for us so we could be set free. How can we thank you? We cannot begin to comprehend what he did to save us from Satan. All we can do is say thank you.

HIS BLOOD

^{39}There was a Roman army officer standing there in front of Jesus. When he saw the way Jesus died, he said, "This man really was God's Son!"

^{42}It was already getting late. It was Preparation Day, which was the day before the sabbath. ^{43}Joseph came. He was from the town of Arimathea. He was a very important member of the Jewish Council. He was expecting the kingdom of God, too. He dared to go in to Pilate and ask for the body of Jesus. ^{44}Pilate was surprised that Jesus had already died. He called for the army officer to ask him whether Jesus had been dead for a long time. ^{45}When Pilate found out from the officer that Jesus was dead, he gave the body to Joseph. ^{46}Joseph bought a linen cloth. He took the body down from the cross and wrapped it in the linen cloth. Then he laid the body of Jesus into a tomb which he had previously cut out of solid rock. He rolled a stone to cover the entrance of the tomb.

PRAYER

Lord, it was now over. Jesus had done it all. So, as they buried his body, he was at rest in paradise ready to return to that body victorious. Oh, what he went through for us because we sin. Our souls cry out thank you.

K. M. Haddad

Mark 15:33-39, 42-46

WEEK 35

HIS BODY

¹When the sabbath day had passed, Mary (the one from Magdala), Mary (the mother of James), and Salome bought some sweet-smelling spices. They wanted to rub this on the body of Jesus. ²It was now very early on Sunday morning. The sun had not come up yet. They were going to the tomb, ³saying to one another, "Who will roll away the stone for us from the entrance of the tomb?" ⁴(The stone was very large.) But, they looked up and saw that the stone was already rolled away! ⁵They walked into the tomb. They saw an angel sitting on the right side. He was wearing a long, white robe. They were stunned.

⁶But the angel said to them, "Don't be alarmed! You are looking for Jesus from Nazareth, who was nailed to the cross. He is not here. He has risen from death! Look at the place where they laid him! ⁷Now, go tell his followers that he will go ahead of you to the land of Galilee. You will see him there, just as he told you. Tell Peter, too."

⁸The women left the tomb. They ran away. They were trembling. They were shocked. They didn't say anything to anyone, because they were afraid.

PRAYER

Lord, they were shocked that Jesus had done exactly what he said he would do. They were shocked he had walked out of his tomb to live forever. Lord, we read your word over and over and claim we would have never doubted. But how easy it is to doubt when surrounded by strong-willed unbelievers. Forgive our arrogance in our own faith and help our faith grow as high as the stars.

HIS BLOOD

^{9}When Jesus came back to life early Sunday morning, he appeared first to Mary (the one from Magdala; Jesus had forced seven demons to leave her.). ^{10}Jesus' friends were crying; they were so sad. She went and told them. ^{11}When they heard that Jesus was alive and that he had been seen by Mary, they didn't believe it.

^{12}After these things, while two more of them were walking to a field, Jesus used a different form to appear to them. ^{13}They went back and told this to the other followers, but the followers didn't believe them, either.

^{14}Finally, Jesus appeared to the eleven apostles when they were sitting at the table. He rebuked them, because their hearts were hard and they did not have faith. They did not believe those who had seen him after he came back to life.

^{15}Jesus said to them, "When you have gone into the whole world, proclaim the Good News to all mankind. ^{16}The person who believes it and is immersed will be saved, but the person who doesn't believe it will be condemned.

The Lord's Supper: 52 Readings with Prayers

PRAYER

Lord, after his death and now in his glorious body, Jesus appeared to many people in different forms. You have promised to give us a glorious body like Jesus' after we die. Let death come, oh God. Then comes the victory. Victory in Jesus. Thank you.

Mark 16:1-16

WEEK 36

HIS BODY

[19] Jesus' followers did exactly as Jesus told them. They prepared the Passover meal. [20] When evening came, Jesus sat down at the table with his twelve followers

[26] While they were eating, Jesus took bread and gave thanks. He broke off some of the bread and gave it to his followers. He said, "Take it and eat it. This bread is my body." [27] Then he took a cup. He gave thanks to God for it and gave it to them. He said, "All of you, drink from it. [28] This is my blood which I am pouring out for many people for the forgiveness of sins. It shows the new covenant which God has made with man. [29] I tell you, from now on, I will never drink this fruit of the vine again, until that day when I drink it new with you in my Father's kingdom." [30] Then they sang a song of praise and went out to Olive Mountain.

PRAYER

Today, Lord, we eat that meal with Jesus as they did long ago. Thank you for giving us something this special to help us along in never forgetting all Jesus did to redeem us, to ransom us from Satan. Never will we take for granted this quiet time of eating that last supper with you each week. You loved us so. We love you too. And will always love you.

HIS BLOOD

³¹Then Jesus said to them, "Tonight all of you will be ashamed of me. This is written: 'I will strike the shepherd, and the flock of sheep will be scattered.'

³²However, after I rise from death, I will go ahead of you to the land of Galilee."

PRAYER

Oh God, we come together to worship you and declare to each other that we will never be ashamed of you, we will never run from you. The one we are ashamed of us ourselves. Our faith is weak compared to what it should be. But eating this weekly last supper with you helps. Thank you for this reminder of what you did to bring us back to you, our Creator.

Matthew 26:19, 26-30

WEEK 37

HIS BODY

[7]During Jesus' human life, he offered prayers to God. Once, with strong cries and tears, Jesus asked God to save him from death.

[36]Then Jesus and his followers went to a place called Gethsemane. Jesus said to them, "Sit here while I go over there and pray."

[37]He took Peter and the two sons of Zebedee with him. He began to feel sad and depressed. [38]Then he said to them, "My soul is full of sorrow; I am going to die! Stay here and be watchful with me." [39]Then Jesus went forward a short distance and bowed down to pray. He said, "My Father, if it is possible, take this cup of suffering away from me—but what You want is more important than what I want."

PRAYER

Lord, Satan never let up. He tried everything near the end to get you to change your mind. He had mankind in his clutches and did not want to lose us. He pressured Jesus with fear and dread, pain and agony, lies and taunts. How you dreaded becoming us with all our sins. You had to be all the murderers, all the rapists, all the torturers, all the cheaters, all the liars, all the enviers, all of every kind of sinner since the beginning of mankind.

How could anyone bear the load? Thank you for not breaking under the load of our sins. Thank you and thank you again.

HIS BLOOD

⁴⁰Then Jesus came to his followers. He found them sleeping. He asked Peter, "So, were you not strong enough to stay awake with me for just one hour!? ⁴¹Watch and pray for strength against temptation. The spirit is willing, but the body is weak."

⁴²Jesus went away the second time. He prayed, "My Father, if this must happen, and I must drink the cup of suffering, if this is what You want, let it be." ⁴³Again, Jesus came and found them sleeping. Their eyes were very tired. ⁴⁴He left them again. The third time he prayed the same prayer. ⁴⁵Then Jesus came to his followers and asked them, "Are you still sleeping and resting!? Listen, the time has come—I am now being handed over into the hands of sinful men! ⁴⁶Get up, we must go. Look! The one who turned against me is near!"

PRAYER

Lord, the human side of Jesus desperately needed his friends when Satan was tempting him so hard to back out and leave us in Satan's clutches forever. Lord, when people taunt you, help us wake up out of our sleep and stand up for you. After all you did to set us free from Satan, we owe you our life, our soul, our being.

K. M. Haddad

Hebrews 5:7a; Matthew 26:36-46

WEEK 38

HIS BODY

⁴⁷While Jesus was still speaking, Judas, one of the twelve apostles, came. There was a large crowd with him. They had come from the most important priests and the elders of the Jewish people. They had clubs and swords. ⁴⁸Judas, the betrayer, had given them the signal to arrest the one he would kiss. ⁴⁹Judas went immediately to Jesus and said, "Greetings, Rabbi!" Then Judas kissed him.

⁵⁰But Jesus said to him, "Friend, do what you came for!" Then the men who came with Judas reached out and grabbed Jesus. ⁵¹Suddenly, one of the men with Jesus reached for his sword and pulled it out. He struck the high priest's slave, cutting off his ear.

⁵²Then Jesus said, "Put your sword back in its place! Everyone who uses violence will die by violence.

PRAYER

Lord, right to the end, Jesus called Judas his friend. Your Bible tells us Jesus was the friend of sinners. Help us be the friend of sinners without participating in their sin. Help us be examples to them without acting superior. Jesus was so great a friend to sinners, he died for them, for all of us. Your love baffles us. We stretch our minds to comprehend you. We stretch our souls to be like you. We stretch our hearts to you, our everlasting friend. Forever, thank you.

HIS BLOOD

⁵³Don't you think I could call on my heavenly Father for help!? He would bring more than twelve legions of angels here! ⁵⁴But how could the Scriptures come true, if this arrest did not happen!?"

⁵⁵At that moment, Jesus said this to the crowd: "Why did you come out here to get me with swords and clubs!? Do you think I am a criminal!? I was sitting in the temple courtyard every day teaching. You did not arrest me there. ⁵⁶All this happened to make the writings of the prophets come true." Then all of Jesus' followers left him. They ran away.

PRAYER

Jesus was in control, Lord. He was always in control. One moment he was teaching his apostles, the next moment he was challenging the mob. The angels were on stand-by in heaven to come whisk him out of danger. But to be victorious, Jesus knew he had to have something to be victorious over and that something was Satan and death and the punishment for our sins. Thank you for staying strong when we were so weak.

Matthew 26:47-56

WEEK 39

HIS BODY

⁵⁷After they arrested Jesus, they brought him to Caiaphas, the high priest. The teachers of the law and the Jewish elders were gathered there.

⁵⁹The most important priests and the whole Jewish Council were trying to find some men who would give false evidence against Jesus, so that they could put him to death. ⁶⁰But they didn't find many people to come forward to tell believable lies. Finally, two men came forward. ⁶¹They claimed, "This man said, 'I am able to destroy God's temple sanctuary and build it again in three days!' "

⁶²The high priest stood up and asked Jesus, "Will you give no answer to what they say against you—is it true!?" ⁶³Jesus continued to be silent.

PRAYER

Lord, they thought that, if they destroyed Jesus' body, they would be destroying him. How they hated anyone who was more popular than them, even if he was God. But that is why you came in a body; to show mankind how people were treating God. Even today people do not accept what you say in your Bible and change it around to suit themselves. A little bit of that lurks in our souls as Satan says again as he did to Eve, "You can be as smart as God." Thank you for standing tall and true in order to die for us in our place.

HIS BLOOD

The high priest said to him, "By the living God, I hereby force you: You must answer! Tell us if you are the Messiah, the Son of God!"

⁶⁴Jesus said to him, "Yes, I AM. Nevertheless, I tell you, from now on, you will see me 'sitting at the right side of God.' I will be coming on the clouds of the sky.' "

⁶⁵Then the high priest ripped his clothes and he cried out, "He has said an evil thing against God! Why do we need any more witnesses!? Listen, you have just heard him say this evil thing! ⁶⁶What do you think!?"

They answered, "He is guilty! He must die!" ⁶⁷Then they spit in Jesus' face. They hit him with their fists. Some of them slapped him. ⁶⁸They said, "Prophesy for us, you Messiah! Let God tell you which one of us hit you!"

PRAYER

Lord, the priests spit at Jesus. The priests hit Jesus with their fists. The priests slapped Jesus. The priests mocked Jesus. They thought God wanted them to treat Jesus that way. Lord, help us examine ourselves this day. Would we have been among them? Our sins nailed him to the cross. How can we thank you enough for doing all you did to save us from Satan.

The Lord's Supper: 52 Readings with Prayers

Matthew 26:57-68

WEEK 40

HIS BODY

¹¹Jesus stood in front of the governor. The governor asked him, "Are you the King of the Jews?"

Jesus answered, "Yes."

¹²The most important priests and the Jewish elders accused Jesus, but Jesus gave no answer. ¹³Then Pilate said to him, "Don't you hear how many charges they are bringing against you!?" ¹⁴But Jesus didn't even say a word. The governor was very surprised.

¹⁵Every year at the Passover Feast, the governor always set one prisoner free, whomever the crowd wanted. ¹⁶This time, they had a well-known prisoner named Jesus Barabbas. ¹⁷Therefore, when the people gathered, Pilate said to them, "Whom do you want me to set free? Jesus Barabbas or the Jesus who is called Messiah?"

¹⁸(Pilate knew that they had handed Jesus over to him because of jealousy.) ¹⁹While Pilate was sitting on the judgment seat, his wife sent a message to him. It said, "Have nothing to do with that innocent man! Last night in a dream, I suffered many things because of him!"

PRAYER

Lord, Pilate wanted to do what was right. His wife wanted him to do what was right. But Jesus' enemies knew everyone has their price, and Pilot's price was to keep his job. Lord, help us from this point on, to never betray you but declare you our Savior.

HIS BLOOD

[20]The most important priests and the Jewish elders persuaded the crowds to ask Pilate for Barabbas. They wanted to destroy Jesus. [21]The governor asked them, "Which of the two men do you want me to set free?" They answered, "Barabbas!"

[22]Pilate asked them, "Then what should I do with Jesus, the one who is called Messiah!?" They all answered, "Nail him to a cross!"

[23]But Pilate asked, "Why? What crime has Jesus done!?" But they continued yelling even more, "Nail him to a cross!"

[24]Pilate saw that he was getting nowhere—only more trouble. He took some water and washed his hands in front of the crowd. He said, "I am not responsible for this man's death—you are!" [25]All the people answered, "We accept that responsibility for us and for our children!"

[26]Then he set Barabbas free for them. After beating Jesus with whips, Pilate handed him over to be nailed to a cross.

²⁷Then the governor's soldiers took Jesus into the Roman fortress. The whole group gathered around Jesus. ²⁸They took off his clothes and dressed him with a long, red robe. ²⁹They used thorny branches to make a crown. Then they put it on his head. They put a stick in his right hand. They kneeled down before him and made fun of him, saying, "Hail, O King of the Jews!" ³⁰They spit on him. They took the stick and began to hit him on the head. ³¹When they finished making fun of him, they took off the long robe and dressed him with his own clothes. Then they led him away to nail him to a cross.

PRAYER

Lord, the crown of thorns was not stripped clean and folded into a perfect circle. It was spring time. His crown had leaves on it and perhaps even a few flowers. His crown looked like the laurel crown of Olympic winners and even Caesar himself. All but the thorns. How his crown hurt. You promised to give us a crown as kings and priests in your kingdom. Sometimes they hurt. Help us wear them proudly, even when they hurt.

Matthew 27:11-31

WEEK 41

HIS BODY

²⁷Then the governor's soldiers took Jesus into the Roman fortress. The whole group gathered around Jesus. ²⁸They took off his clothes and dressed him with a long, red robe. ²⁹They used thorny branches to make a crown. Then they put it on his head. They put a stick in his right hand. They kneeled down before him and made fun of him, saying, "Hail, O King of the Jews!" ³⁰They spit on him. They took the stick and began to hit him on the head. ³¹When they finished making fun of him, they took off the long robe and dressed him with his own clothes. Then they led him away to nail him to a cross.

³²As they were going out of Jerusalem, they found a man from the city of Cyrene. His name was Simon. They forced him to carry Jesus' cross. ³³They came to a place called Golgotha. (This means 'The Place of the Skull.') ³⁴They gave Jesus some wine. (A drug for pain was mixed with it.) When he had tasted it, he refused to drink it. ³⁵Then they nailed him to a cross. The soldiers gambled to see who would get Jesus' clothes. ³⁶They sat there watching him. ³⁷At the top of the cross, they wrote the reason for his punishment in these words:

"THIS IS JESUS, THE KING OF THE JEWS."

PRAYER

Lord, by this time, Jesus should have already been dead. He's been forced to stay awake all night and endure an illegal middle-of-the night arrest and trial, and endure beating by the priests, and endure beating by the soldiers. Only with the strongest will did Jesus stay alive. He had to so they could nail his body to a wretched cross. How can we thank you for offering your body in exchange for our souls?

HIS BLOOD

[38] Along with Jesus, two criminals were nailed to crosses. One was on his right. The other was on his left. [39] The people who were passing by shook their heads and said terrible things to Jesus. [40] They said, "You are the one who was going to destroy the temple sanctuary and build it again in three days! Since you are the Son of God, save yourself! Come on down from the cross!"

[41] In the same way, the most important priests, the teachers of the law, and the Jewish elders made fun of Jesus. They continued to say, [42] "He saved other people, but he cannot save himself! He is the King of Israel; let him come down from the cross now! Then we will believe in him! [43] He trusts in God; let God rescue him now, if He wants him. Jesus did say, 'I am the Son of God.' "

PRAYER

Lord, it was our blood that should have been drained from our body that day, not yours. It was our lungs that should have screamed for air, our wounds that should have writhed in pain, our heart that should have burst that day so long ago. How can we thank you for taking our place? We will spend eternity thanking you.

The Lord's Supper: 52 Readings with Prayers

Matthew 27: 27-43

WEEK 42

HIS BODY

⁴⁵There was darkness over the whole land from noon until three o'clock in the afternoon. ⁴⁶At about three o'clock, Jesus shouted this loudly: "Eli, Eli, lema sa-bak-tha-ni!?" (This means: "My God, my God, why did you abandon me!?") ⁴⁷Some of the men standing there heard this. They said, "This man is calling for Elijah."

⁴⁸One of them quickly ran and got a sponge. He soaked it in some sour wine. Then he put it on the end of a long stick and gave Jesus a drink. ⁴⁹The other men said, "Leave him alone. Let's see if Elijah will come and save him!"

⁵⁰Again, Jesus cried out very loudly. Then he died.

PRAYER

Lord, we hear that giving a drink to a person in shock will kill them. Is this what Jesus was doing? Was he through? Had he faced down Satan and won? Had he fulfilled all the law and the prophecies? As the final drops of blood flowed out of his body, did his heart break? Lord, we are so sorry for all our everyday sins ~ especially those of failing to do good works and sitting home instead. We are sorry. Thank you for saving us from the punishment for our sins.

HIS BLOOD

⁵¹Then, look, the curtain in the temple sanctuary was split into two parts—from the top to the bottom. The earth shook. Large rocks broke apart. ⁵²⁻⁵³(Tombs were opened. After Jesus rose from the grave, many holy people who had died were raised from death, too. They left their tombs and went into Jerusalem. They appeared to many people.)

⁵⁴A Roman army officer and some of his men were guarding the body of Jesus. When they saw the earthquake and the other things that happened, they were very frightened. They said, "This man really was God's Son."

PRAYER

Lord, how could Jesus' enemies not know? He had made people's eyes new again, replaced the arms and legs of the maimed, given new skin and bones to lepers. The sky was black for three hours in the middle of the day, there was an earthquake, the most secret part of the temple was exposed to the world when the curtain tore in two, and dead people were coming back to life. How could they all not know? They did know. How can people in our town be out there shopping, eating, going to games, or sleeping in instead of being here with you at your table? Lord, help us lead them to your cross.

Matthew 27:45-54

K. M. Haddad

WEEK 43

HIS BODY

¹After the sabbath day, when Sunday morning was dawning, Mary (the one from Magdala) and the other Mary were on their way to look at the grave. ²Suddenly, there was a great earthquake. An angel of the Lord came down from heaven. He went to the large stone and rolled it away. Then the angel sat on top of it. ³His appearance was shining like lightning. His clothes were as white as snow. ⁴The men who were guarding the tomb trembled with fear; they acted as if they were dead men.

⁵The angel said to the women, "Don't be afraid. I know you are looking for Jesus, who was nailed to the cross. ⁶He is not here! He was raised from death, just as he said.

PRAYER

Our God, you make wonderous promises and you keep them. We read your promises and then blithely go on our way. We claim to believe your promises, but don't. You promised we would come back to life when we die, but we cry and panic and beg God to not let us die. Not let us into your glorious home? Lord, we're trying to believe. Help our unbelief.

HIS BLOOD

"Come, look at the place where he lay. [7]Go quickly and tell his followers: 'Jesus has been raised from death! Listen, he will go ahead of you to the land of Galilee. You will see him there.' Remember, I told you."

[8]The women left the tomb quickly. They were afraid, yet very happy. They ran to tell Jesus' followers. [9]Suddenly, Jesus met them. He said, "Greetings!" They went to him, held onto his feet, and worshiped him. [10]Then Jesus said to them, "Don't be afraid. Go, tell my brothers that they must leave for Galilee. They will see me there."

PRAYER

Lord, not only did Jesus' apostles not believe he came back to life, but they refused to leave Jerusalem and go back north to Galilee like he told them to over and over. They stayed in hiding in Jerusalem and Jesus had to walk through their wall because their door was locked. Sometimes, Lord, we refuse to leave our hiding place ~ which is often the church building ~ to tell others of you. Lord, give us the courage of Jesus.

Matthew 28:1-10

WEEK 44

HIS BODY

³But all have turned away. Together, everyone has become rotten. None of them does anything good —not even one person!

O Yahweh, hear my prayer! Listen to my cry for mercy! Come help me because You are loyal and righteous. ²Don't put me, Your servant, on trial because no one alive is innocent in Your presence. I love Your teachings....

³But everyone has turned away. Together, everybody has become filthy. None of them are doing anything good — not a single person!

¹⁵But You, O Lord, are a God who shows mercy and who is kind. You don't become angry quickly. You have great love and faithfulness.

PRAYER

Father, everyone sins. How can you be so patient with us? Our sins make us your enemy. But we keep committing them because we think your patience will never end. Most of our sins are of attitude ~ jealousy, impatience and so on ~ and of neglecting doing to good things you commanded us to do. We think you won't mind. Help us this day admit and examine our faults and do away with them. These are the sins that drove the spikes into Jesus' body.

HIS BLOOD

[14]Your kingdom is built on what is right and fair. Constant love and truth accompany all You do.

[76]Please comfort me with Your constant love, as You promised me, Your servant. [77]Have mercy on me, so that I may live.

[25]My enemies insult me. They look at me and shake their heads.

[20]He will protect my very bones; not one of them will be broken.

PRAYER

Our God, Jesus said the world hated him so the world will hate us too if we follow him. We will be insulted because he was. We will be lied about because he was. We will be injured because he was.
But you will protect us and give us comfort. Such love as dying on the cross goes with us everywhere. Make us more loving.

Psalm 14:3; Psalm 143:1-2; Psalm 53:3; Psalm 86:15; Psalm 89:14; Psalm 119:77; Psalm 109:25; Psalm 34:20

WEEK 45

HIS BODY

¹My God, my God, why did you abandon me? You are too far away to save me. You are too far away to hear my moans....

⁶But I am like a worm instead of a man. Men make fun of me. The people look down on me. ⁷Everyone who looks at me laughs. They stick out their tongues at me. They shake their heads. ⁸They say: "Let him turn to Yahweh for help! Let Him rescue him! If He likes you, maybe He will deliver you!?"

¹³They open their jaws at me. Like hungry, roaring lions. ¹⁴My strength is all gone, like water poured out onto the ground. All of my bones are out of joint.
My heart is like wax. It has melted inside me"

PRAYER

Lord, we can hardly understand the spirit agony Jesus went through on the cross. The weight of becoming every sinner in the history of the world must have been unbearable. But he did it. He took the sins of every killer, every kidnapper, every rapist, every torturer, every impatient person, every liar. It was unbearable, but he bore it and the punishment that came with it. How can we thank you for taking our place?

HIS BLOOD

[15] My strength has dried up like a piece of broken pottery. My tongue sticks to the roof of my mouth. You laid me in the dust of death. [16] A gang of wrongdoers has trapped me. Like a pack of dogs, they have surrounded me. They bit my arms and legs.

[17] I have been stripped. People look and stare at me. [18] They divided my clothes among them, and they gambled for my clothing.

[20] He will protect His very bones; not one of them will be broken.

PRAYER

Lord, during those last hours on the cross, Satan threw everything at Jesus he possibly could. Like Jesus' false accusers, Satan was afraid of Jesus and his power. Jesus' power was to forgive as though we had never committed those sins and left undone those good works we should have done. We are so sorry for our sins that nailed Jesus to the cross.

Psalm 22:1, 6-8, 13-18; Psalm 34:20

WEEK 46

HIS BODY

K. M. Haddad

O God, be merciful to me, because You are a loving God. Because You are always ready to be merciful, wipe out all of my rebellions. ²Wash me thoroughly of my guilt, and cleanse me from my sin. ³I admit my rebellions; my sin is continually right there in front of me. ⁴I have sinned against You, and You alone. I have done wrong in Your sight. So, You are proved right when You sentence me. You are fair when You judge me. ⁵Listen, I was brought forth into a world of wrongdoing. In the surroundings of sin did my mother conceive me. ⁶Listen, You want me to be completely honest. So, teach me true wisdom.

⁷Purge me with hyssop, and I will be pure. Wash me; then I will be whiter than snow. ⁸Let me hear sounds of joy and gladness. Let the bones that You crushed be happy again. ⁹Turn Your face away from my sins. Wipe out all of my guilt!

PRAYER

Father, our guilt is so great. Oh, we don't kill, but we steal little things at work, we lie in order to save people's feelings, we break your commandments when we speed, we insult you when we stay home or go out for entertainment instead of visiting people who need us. We lay our sins before you, praying for your forgiveness which only became possible at the cross. Wash us in Jesus' blood and make our souls white and pure.

HIS BLOOD

^{10}Create a pure heart for me, O God. Please renew a solid spirit within me. ^{11}Do not send me away from Your presence! Don't take Your holy spirit away from me. ^{12}Give me back the joy of Your salvation.
Grant me a volunteering attitude to keep me going.

^{13}Then I will teach Your ways to those who rebel.
And, sinners will turn back to You. ^{14}O God, deliver me from the guilt of murder! O God, You are the One who saves me. I will sing loudly about Your righteousness. ^{15}O Lord, let me speak, so that I may praise You.

PRAYER

Lord, we are so embarrassed over our sins. Sometimes we pretend we did not do them. Other times we say they aren't so bad when we know they are. Sometimes we give in to our friends so they will still like us and the pangs of guilt haunt us. Lord, we are trying to do better; help us try harder. You did so much to save us from Satan. Help us live a life of gratitude for all you did for us.

Psalm 51:1-15

WEEK 47

HIS BODY

³I'm tired of calling out for help. My throat is sore. My eyes are strained from looking for my God. ⁴The people who hate me for no reason outnumber the hairs on my head. Those who desire to destroy me are powerful. My enemies are liars.

⁶O Lord, Yahweh of the armies of heaven, don't let those who hope in You be disgraced because of me. Don't let those who seek You be ashamed because of me. ⁷For Your sake, I carry this blame. My face is covered with shame.

PRAYER

Lord, we too are ashamed of our sins ~ sins of attitude and sins of neglect mostly. We pretend we aren't so bad. We pretend our sins are not really sinful. May our sins never be the reason anyone falls away from you. May we face our sins for what they are, be ashamed, and become more like you.

HIS BLOOD

⁸I am like a stranger to my brothers. I am like a foreigner to the sons of my mother. ⁹The fire which I feel for Your House burns within me! The insults of the people who were insulting You fell on me. ¹⁶O Yahweh,

answer me because Your constant love is so good. In Your great compassion, turn to me.
[17]Don't hide Your face from me, Your servant.
I'm in trouble. Please answer me quickly.

[19]You how I am insulted, shamed, and disgraced; all of my enemies are before You. [20]Insults have broken my heart; I am sick. I looked for sympathy, but there was none. I looked for comforters, but I found no one.

PRAYER

Oh, Lord, those people who insulted you then are still insulting you through us. Those who shamed and disgraced you then are still shaming and disgracing you through us. May we feel honored to be treated the way people treated you. Help us to never betray you.

Psalm 69:3-4, 6-9, 16-17, 19-20

WEEK 48

HIS BODY

O my soul, praise Yahweh! All my inner being, praise His holy Name! ²O my soul, praise Yahweh. Don't forget all of His kindnesses. ³He forgives all of my sins.

He heals all of my diseases. ⁴He redeems my life from the grave. He crowns me with constant love and mercy. ⁵He satisfies my desires with good things.
He makes me feel young again, like the eagle.

⁶Yahweh does what is right and fair for all who are oppressed by others....Yahweh shows mercy, and He is kind. He does not become angry quickly, and He has great, constant love. ⁹He will not always reprimand us.
He will not be angry forever. ¹⁰He has not punished us as our sins deserved to be punished. He has not repaid us for the evil that we have done.

PRAYER

Lord God, it is we who should have been on the cross that day. We deserved the punishment that day. After all, they were our sins, not Jesus'. But you had mercy on us and made it possible to snatch us from Satan, the accuser, and to forgive us. How you longed to have mercy on us. How can we thank you enough?

HIS BLOOD

¹¹As high as the sky is above the earth, so great is His constant love for those who revere Him. ¹²He has taken our sins away from us, as far as the east is from the west. ¹³Yahweh has mercy upon those who revere Him, as a father has mercy on his children.

¹⁴He knows how we were made. He remembers that we are dust. ¹⁵Human life is like grass. Man grows like a flower in the field. ¹⁶After the wind blows it, the flower is gone. There is no sign of where it once was. ¹⁷But Yahweh's constant love for those who revere Him continues forever and ever. And, His fairness continues to grandchildren and beyond.

PRAYER

Thank you, Lord, for understanding our weaknesses. We are so ashamed of them. But you look on us from heaven as little children and love us anyway. Jesus' blood washed our sins away and you see us as never having sinned. You see us as pure and innocent. It is your sacrifice in our place that made it possible. Thank you, Lord, for making us better than we are.

Psalm 103:1-17

WEEK 49

HIS BODY

I will exalt You, O my God, the King. I will bless Your Name forever and ever. ²I will bless You every day. Yes, I will praise Your Name forever and ever.

³Yahweh is great. He is worthy of our praise. No one can fully understand how great He is. ⁴Each generation will extol what You have done. They will retell Your mighty deeds. ⁵They will proclaim the glorious splendor of Your majesty. And, I will think about Your wonders. ⁶They will tell of the awesome things that You do. And, I will declare how great You are. ⁷They will celebrate the fame of Your great goodness. They will sing about Your fairness.

⁸Yahweh is kind, and He shows mercy. He does not easily become angry. Instead, He is full of constant love. ⁹Yahweh is good to everyone. And, He is merciful to everything He has made. ¹⁰O Yahweh, everything You have made will thank You. Those who follow You will bless You. ¹¹They will tell about the glory of Your kingdom. And, they will speak of Your power, ¹² so that all men may come to realize Your power. And, they will know the glorious majesty of Your kingdom. ¹³Your kingdom will continue forever.
And, You will rule throughout all generations.

PRAYER

We praise you, God of our souls. You have had mercy on us because you are Love. You wanted to see us as pure as the day you made us and, because of the body that was pierced and the blood that was drained from that body, you made it happen. Oh, Lord, how can you do all you have done for us? How can our gratitude measure up to what you deserve? We will thank you for eternity.

HIS BLOOD

Yahweh will keep all of His promises. He takes care of everything He has made by His constant love. [14]Yahweh helps those who have been defeated. He takes care of those who are in trouble. [15]In hope, all eyes look to You for food. And, You give it to them at the proper time. [16]You open Your hand, and You satisfy the appetite of all living things.

[17]Everything that Yahweh does is right. With His constant love, He takes care of all He has made. [18]Yahweh is near everyone who calls out to Him, to all who truly call upon Him. [19]He gives those who revere Him what they desire. He listens to their cries for help, and He saves them. [20]Yahweh protects everyone who loves Him. But He will destroy all evil people.

[21]I will praise Yahweh. Let everyone bless His holy Name forever and ever!

PRAYER

Father of Mercies, our unworthy souls rise from this room to your throne room of holiness. We worship you for all you did to save us from Satan. Sometimes we wander from you and you run after us calling out, "Come back. Come back to me. I just want to save you." You bought us back from Satan with blood. And so, we worship you now and forever.

Psalm 148:1-21

WEEK 50

HIS BODY

....Jesus loves us. He bled, setting us free from our sins. He formed us into a kingdom. We are priests to God, his Father.

[8]"I am the A and the Z" says the Lord God. He is the One who is, who was, and who will be. He is all-powerful.

[13]There was one like the Son of Man among them. He was dressed with a very long robe. He wore a golden belt around his waist. [14]His head and his hair were white, white like wool or like snow. His eyes were like the flame of a fire. [15]His feet were like shining brass, when glowing in an oven. His voice was loud, like the rushing sound of much water. [16]He had seven stars in his right hand. A sword, sharp on both edges, was coming out of his mouth. His face looked like the sun, when it shines its brightest.

[17]When I saw him, I fell down at his feet as if I were dead. Then he put his right hand on me and said, "Don't be afraid! I am the First and the Last. [18]I am the one who is alive. I was dead, but, look, I am alive forever and ever! I have the keys to death and Hades. [9]They sang a new song:

"You are worthy to take the scroll

and to open its seals,
because you were killed.
You used your blood to
buy back people for God
from every tribe, language, people, and nation."
"The Lamb who was killed is worthy to receive
power, wealth, wisdom, strength,
honor, glory, and praise!"

PRAYER

Oh to be with you in heaven, the home of our soul. Lord, hasten the day when we may join you there. Help us not fear death but look forward to the day we will close our eyes here and open them to see you face to face. Jesus, who once was covered with our sins made it all possible. Our souls rise to you and thank you forever.

HIS BLOOD

[7]There was a war in heaven. Michael and his angels fought against the dragon. The dragon and his angels fought back. [8]But the dragon was not strong enough. There was no place left for the dragon and his angels in heaven anymore. [9]The large dragon was thrown out. (This is the old snake who is the same as the one called the Devil, Satan. He is the one who fools the whole world.) He was thrown down to the earth. He and his angels were **thrown out.** [10]I heard a loud voice in heaven say: **"Now the salvation,** the power, the

kingdom of our God, and the authority of His Christ have come, because the accuser of our brothers has been **thrown out**. He always accuses them in front of our God day and night. ¹¹But they have defeated him because of the Lamb's **blood**

PRAYER

Lord, the final victory over Satan and his angels came at the cross. The final victory to unlock the gates where Satan held us as his slaves came at the cross. Now Satan, the great accuser, is helpless because you became the Great Forgiver at the cross. We are now washed clean of all sins in your blood. We will praise and thank you to the end of eternity.

Revelation 1:8, 13-18; Revelation 5:9, 12b; Revelation 12:7-11b;

WEEK 51

HIS BODY

³The Good News is about God's Son who, on the physical side, was a descendant of David. ⁴But, long ago, it was planned that our Lord Jesus Christ be the Son of God with power in a holy, divine way. How? By rising from death!

¹⁰"No one is righteous—not even one person.... ²³because everyone has sinned and is far away from God's glory. ²⁴But, with God's gracious love, we are made right with God through Christ Jesus who sets us free. And, all of this is free! ²⁵God offered Christ as a sacrifice. When Christ died, this became the way that sins are taken away—if we believe. This showed God's justice, too. God passed over sins which had been committed before this time. He let it go.

²⁵Jesus was handed over to die for our sins. He was raised from death to make us right with God.

PRAYER

Father, what comfort to know that the blood of Christ covered sins which had been committed before his crucifixion. We think of Noah, Abraham, Joseph, David, Isaiah, Jonah ~ so many of our heroes. All saved because of Jesus whose blood covered the sins of all mankind from the creation to far into the future. How powerful your blood. Thank you for snatching us from Satan and setting us free to live with you forever.

HIS BLOOD

[14]We know that the law is spiritual, but I am not. I'm human—sold under sin! [15]I don't understand what is happening to me: I don't always do what I really want to do. Instead, I am always doing what I actually hate. [16]Since I am doing what I don't want to do, I am agreeing with the law, that the law is right. [17]But now, I am not the one who is doing this anymore. No, it is the sin which is living in me. [18]I know that good does not live in me. (I mean, in my human nature.) I am ready and willing to do good, but I can't do it. [19]I am not doing the good that I actually want to do. Instead, I continue doing something evil that I really don't want to do. [20]Since I am doing what I really don't want to do, it is not me doing it anymore—it is the sin which is living in me that is doing it!

[21]So, I find this principle: When I want to do something good, evil is controlling me. [22]My inner self happily agrees with the law of God. [23]However, I see a different law in my body, making war with the law of my mind. It is making me a prisoner to the sinful law which is in my body. [24]I am a miserable man. Who will help me escape this body of death!? [25]Thank God, I can escape through Jesus Christ, our Lord.

PRAYER

Lord, we come together with others to remember the last supper and to take it with you again. But when we do, we tend to forget we are sinners. We pray together and sing together and everything seems to right. Help us take time as we worship you to admit our sins and determine to do away with them. Your blood made it possible. But it is so hard. We decide to do better on Sunday, then don't on Monday. Give us strength to become more like our Savior. Keep our eyes on you and our soul at your feet in worship.

Romans 1:3-4; Romans 3:10, 23-25; Romans 6:25; Romans 7:14-25a

WEEK 52

HIS BODY

⁸Look, I am going to bring forth My Servant called "The Branch."... Yahweh of the armies of heaven. 'And, in one day, I will take away the sin of this land!'

⁹Rejoice greatly, O you people of Zion! Shout for joy, O you people of Jerusalem. Behold, your King is coming to you! He does what is right, and he will have salvation in himself. He is gentle and riding on a donkey, even upon a young donkey, born of a work animal.

¹²Then I said to them, "If you want to pay me, then pay me. If not, then don't." So, they paid me 30 pieces of silver. ¹³The Always-Present One said to me, "Put them in the temple treasury." (That is how little they thought I was worth.) So, I threw that money at the potter inside the temple of Yahweh.

¹⁰"And, I will pour out a spirit of kindness and mercy upon David's household and the inhabitants in Jerusalem. They will look at Me, the One they have pierced to death. And, they will mourn like someone weeping over the death of an only child. They will be as sad as someone who has lost a firstborn son.

PRAYER

Lord, your Plan to ransom us from Satan began in the Garden of Eden. Step by step you revealed your Plan to your prophets who lived hundreds of years before Jesus. Step by step you made it happen. Glorious day when Jesus finally set us free. How can we thank you enough? We will spend eternity thanking you.

HIS BLOOD

¹God says: "At that time, a fountain will be opened....It will cleanse them of sin and of impurity."

⁶"But someone may ask him: 'Well, what are those deep cuts on your body?'...⁷"O sword, hit My Shepherd!" says Yahweh of the armies of heaven.
"Strike the Shepherd, and the flock will be scattered."

⁶At that time, there will be no light... ⁷It will be a unique day. (The Always-Present One knows when it will happen.) There will be no day or night. At evening time, it will still be light.

⁹Then Yahweh will be King over the whole world. At that time, Yahweh will be recognized as the one true God. And His Name will be the only Name!

PRAYER

Lord, at last Jesus came and fulfilled all the prophecies about him so we could recognize him. At last Jesus came and changed nature through his miracles so we could recognize him. At last in his weakness on the cross, he faced down Satan and grabbed us away from him. The debt had been paid. We became free of guilt because of your blood. Our minds reel trying to understand it all. Our hearts tremble at the thought of all you went through to save us from Satan. Our soul soar to you and worship you, our Lord and our Savior.

Zechariah 3:8b, 9b; Zechariah 9:9; Zechariah 11:12b-13; Zechariah 12:10b-11a; Zechariah 13:1, 6-7b; Zechariah 14:6, 9a

K. M. Haddad

THANK YOU

Thanks for reading my book! I'm so honored that you chose to spend your precious time with my research and studies. You are appreciated. I'm an independent author who relies on my readers to help spread the word about stories you enjoy. Would you take a few minutes to let your friends know on Facebook, Pinterest... wherever you spend your time online?

Also, each honest review at online retailers means a lot to me and helps other readers know if this is a book they might enjoy,

I welcome contact from readers. At my website (below), you can do so. You can also sign up for my newsletter (below) to be notified of half-price books and new releases.

ABOUT THE COMPILER

K. M. Haddad grew up in the cold north and now lives in Arizona where she does not have to shovel sunshine. She basks in 100-degree weather with palm trees, cacti, and a computer with most of the lettering worn off.

Woth a bachelor's degree in English, Bible, and history, from Harding University, she also has a Master's Degree in management and human relations from Abilene Christian University, and part of a Master's Degree in Bible from Harding School of Theology, including Greek studies.

She spends half her day writing, and the other half teaching English over the internet worldwide using the Bible as textbook through World English Institute. She has taught over 7000 Muslims, mostly in the Middle East. Students she has converted to Christianity are in hiding in Afghanistan, Iran, Iraq, Yemen, Jordan, Somalia, Uzbekistan, Tajikistan, and Palestine. "They are my heroes," she says.

In addition to her seventy-seven books, she has written numerous articles for *Gospel Advocate, Twentieth Century Christian, Firm Foundation, Christian Bible Teacher, Christian Woman,* and several world mission publications. Her weekly column, *Little-Known Facts About the Bible,* appeared several years in newspapers in North Carolina and Texas.

K. M. Haddad

BUY YOUR NEXT BOOK NOW

CHRISTIAN LIFE
Applied Christianity: Handbook 500 Good Works
You Can Be a Hero Alone
Worship Changes Since 1st Century + Worship 1sr Century Way
The Best of Alexander Campbell's Millennial Harbinger
Inside the Hearts of Bible Women-Reader+Audio+Leader
The Lord's Supper: 52 Readings with Prayers
http://bit.ly/Christianlife

BIBLE TEXT STUDIES
Revelation: A Love Letter From God
The Holy Spirit: 592 Verses Examined
Was Jesus God? (Why Evil)
365 Life-Changing Scriptures Day by Date
Love Letters of Jesus & His Bride, Ecclesia
Christianity or Islam? The Contrast
The Road to Heaven
http://bit.ly/BibleTexts

FUN BOOKS
Bible Puzzles, Bible Song Book, Bible Numbers
http://bit.ly/BibleFun

TOUCHING GOD SERIES
365 Golden Bible Thoughts: God's Heart to Yours
365 Pearls of Wisdom: God's Soul to Yours
365 Silver-Winged Prayers: Your Spirit to God's
http://bit.ly/TouchingGodSeries

-SURVEY SERIES: EASY BIBLE WORKBOOKS
→Old Testament & New Testament Surveys
→Questions You Have Asked-Part I & II
http://bit.ly/BibleWorkbooks

HISTORICAL RESEARCH BIBLE
for Novel, Screenwriter, Documentary & Thesis Writers
http://bit.ly/32uZkHa

GENEALOGY: How to Climb Your Family Tree Without Falling Out
Volume I & 2: Beginner-Intermediate & Colonial-Medieval
http://bit.ly/GenealogyBeginner-Advanced

CONNECT WITH THE AUTHOR

Website: **https://inspirationsbykatheryn.com**

Facebook:
bit.ly/FacebooksKatherynMaddoxHaddad

Linkedin: **http://bit.ly/KatherynLinkedin**

Twitter: **https://twitter.com/KatherynHaddad**

Pinterest:
https://www.pinterest.com/haddad1940/

Goodreads:
https://www.goodreads.com/katherynmaddoxhaddad

GET A FREE BOOK

Sign up for Katheryn's monthly newsletter with half-price books for the whole family and insider tips on what's coming next.
http://bit.ly/katheryn

JOIN MY DREAM TEAM

Members get the first peek at my newest book and have fun offering me advice sometimes and help me get the word out. Check it out here:
http://bit.ly/KatherynsDreamTeam

K. M. Haddad